Exploring the
EVIDENCE
for
CREATION

Exploring the

EVIDENCE

for

CREATION

HENRY M. MORRIS III

INSTITUTE
for CREATION
RESEARCH

Dallas, Texas
www.icr.org

EXPLORING THE EVIDENCE FOR CREATION
by Henry M. Morris III, D.Min.

First printing: January 2009

ISBN-13: 978-0-932766-93-9
ISBN-10:   0-932766-93-5
Library of Congress Catalog Number: 2008943902

Please visit our website for other books and resources: www.icr.org.

Printed in the United States of America.

CONTENTS

ACKNOWLEDGMENTS

This book is a distillation of nearly four decades of scientific research conducted by the dedicated men and women of the Institute for Creation Research.

Dr. Henry M. Morris, ICR's founder, wrote over 60 books, many more booklets and pamphlets, and literally hundreds of articles during his 36 years "on the job." Early on he was joined by Dr. Duane Gish, who became a renowned debater among colleges and universities—fiercely defending the accuracy of the biblical model for the origin of life, as well as exposing the emptiness of the evolutionary claim of transitional fossils in the geological record.

Other researchers joined the science faculty as word of our work spread. Dr. Steve Austin, considered one of the most knowledgeable creation geologists in the world today, became active as a field geologist for ICR, and began his three-decade research in the Grand Canyon, followed by nearly a decade of active field work on Mount St Helens.

Ken Ham was on the ICR team for several years before he left with our blessing to establish Answers in Genesis and the Creation Museum in Petersburg, Kentucky.

Dr. Larry Vardiman coordinated the groundbreaking project on isotope dating called Radioisotopes and the Age of the Earth (RATE). This eight-year study involved all of the scientific staff at ICR, along with several others with whom ICR had established adjunct relationships.

For the past 10 years, Dr. John Morris, one of the sons of our founder, has served as president of ICR. A geological engineer and former professor, Dr. Morris has written several popular books dealing with the core issues in the creation-evolution debate.

There are many others, of course, who have written articles or books for ICR and whose materials have been adapted for use in this book.

Andrew Snelling, Ph.D.	Frank Sherwin, M.A.
Chris Osborne, Ph.D.	Gary Parker, Ph.D.
D. Russell Humphreys, Ph.D	John Baumgardner, Ph.D.
Daniel C. Criswell, Ph.D.	James J. S. Johnson, J.D.
David A. DeWitt, Ph.D.	Patricia L. Nason, Ph.D.
David Coppedge	Sharon E. Cargo, D.V.M.
Donald DeYoung, Ph.D.	Stephen W. Deckard, Ed.D.
Eddy Miller, Ph.D.	William Hoesch, M.S.

Most of the following material can also be found on our website, www.icr.org. Several years ago, Richard Pferdner, ICR's Director of Internet Ministries, met with me to cast his vision of a broader outreach for ICR on the Internet. His passion for reaching out beyond the normal "borders" of ICR was so infectious that I encouraged him to join the ICR team and help me implement that vision.

Lawrence Ford, ICR's Director of Communications, and his managing editor, Beth Mull, have been instrumental in making sure that the material is readable for most of us. Without their help and the diligence of ICR's technical staff, the instant availability of ICR's archives would be difficult to access.

Rare is the book that is written without any help or encouragement. So it is with this work. The editing, transitional additions, and compilation that have been done, could not have occurred without the skillful hands of so many among the ICR staff and faculty.

I am most grateful to all of them and trust that this abbreviated printed edition of these rich resources will impact the lives of many.

Henry M. Morris III, D.Min.
Chief Executive Officer
Institute for Creation Research
Dallas, Texas

WHY READ THIS BOOK?

"In the beginning, God created...."

Does the God described in the Bible really exist? Is it plausible to believe that an omnipotent, omniscient Being has existed eternally? And did that God really create everything in the universe? Or did everything that exists develop over billions of years as a result of the random interaction of stellar gas?

It is man's nature to question life and the world around him. Who am I? How am I different from the other creatures on earth? Am I just a higher order of animal, just a freak accident of nature's infinite cycle of accidents over billions of years? Could I possibly be created in the image of God, or am I merely the fittest of animals, now able to use everything within my power for my own pleasure? Is my sole purpose in life to fulfill those personal desires—to simply survive—or was I, a member of humanity, designed to serve and glorify something or Someone much greater? Is life an exquisite work of art or a cosmic joke at man's expense?

There are two very different views on these fundamental questions. These views or "worldviews," as they are often called, are belief systems that hold their own presuppositions that we use every day to interpret the meaning of everything around us. Some have suggested that all presuppositions can be summarized by two types of information filters: atheist, which presupposes that God does not and cannot exist, and creationist, which presupposes that God is the originator and sustainer of everything.

Obviously, these two are in diametrical opposition with each other.

Those who presuppose that God does not exist look at everything from a purely naturalistic viewpoint. Everything is to be explained without God in the story. Those who presuppose that God does exist attempt to understand everything in light of what that God has revealed, both in His creation and in the information that God Himself caused to be recorded through human authors over the millennia.

This book rests firmly on a *creationist* worldview.

If the creationist worldview is true, then we should expect to discover real, tangible, and observable evidence that supports the fundamental tenets of that which is believed. In fact, the God of Scripture insists: "Prove me now herewith, saith the LORD of hosts." Indeed, if God does exist, there ought to be plenty of evidence that He exists. If there is no God or gods or some sort of Designer, that should also be clear.

This book presents evidence to validate the creationist worldview.

The answers we seek from the limited experience and knowledge of our own lives are, in fact, freely given by the One who created us. God's very existence is witnessed in the creation, and His immutable truth is clearly proclaimed for all to observe. Even science itself—we might even say, especially science—verifies the hand of a Creator in our universe. The Bible, unique and beautiful in its account of human history from the beginning, becomes our foundational textbook in which we begin our search for truth.

The Bible describes the first humans, Adam and Eve, as nothing less than the personal "hands-on" creation of God, endowed with His unique "image." You and I, the direct descendants of that first pair, bear that same image. If this is so, and man was truly designed by God, then he is loved deeply by Him as well.

The universe, the earth, all life, and especially mankind were created by God. The message of Scripture is undeniable. And as a result of what God has revealed about Himself and what He made, every question that man could ask about life, purpose, and himself is answered in the Bible.

But evidence for God's existence and His special creation abounds not just in the sacred text of Christianity. His existence, His truth, His work are all are clearly seen through science, reason, and nature. The love of God for His creation compelled Him to clearly communicate how important it is that every person know how they were formed and what meaning their lives are to have on earth. As important as the truth of God's creation and His love for man are, why wouldn't He provide evidence from so many realms?

This book will detail the evidence for God and His creation in the following five categories.

- Evidence for God
- Evidence for Truth
- Evidence from Nature
- Evidence from Science
- Evidence from Scripture

Each section provides both the obvious and the challenging, along with suggestions for further study.

May God richly bless you as you explore the evidence for creation.

EVIDENCE *for* GOD

The fool hath said in his heart, There is no God.

Psalm 14:1

EVIDENCE
for
GOD

The best explanation for the cause of the reality we experience is an all-powerful, all-present, all-knowing, and loving God. While absolute proof of the existence of God cannot be realized by any human being, the great weight of evidence, when rationally evaluated, clearly balances the scales heavily in favor of God. We can demonstrate "beyond a reasonable doubt" that "he is, and that he is a rewarder of them that diligently seek him" (Hebrews 11:6).

God has promised numerous times that He will help us understand what He has done for us. Indeed, there are promises that ensure our discovery of God's existence—if we really want to know the truth.

> For I know the thoughts that I think toward you, saith the LORD, thoughts of peace, and not of evil, to give you an expected end. Then shall ye call upon me, and ye shall go and pray unto me, and I will hearken unto you. And ye shall seek me, and find me, when ye shall search for me with all your heart. (Jeremiah 29:11-13)

If that promise is true, we ought to be able to "see" God in the physical world in such a way that knowledge of God would be obvious or "intuitive" through our everyday experience. In fact, that is exactly what God promises.

> For the invisible things of him from the creation of the world are clearly seen, being understood by the things that are made, even his eternal power and Godhead. (Romans 1:20)

Even the "invisible things" are "clearly seen" by what is available to all of us. Are you aware that all of science rests on an "invisible" law of science?

CAUSE AND EFFECT

The most certain and universal of all scientific principles is that of causality, or the law of cause and effect. The implications of this principle have been fought over vigorously in theological and philosophical disciplines, but there is no question of its universal acceptance in the world of experimental science, as well as in ordinary experience.

During the first century A.D., a high-ranking Jewish leader named Saul, from Tarsus, became so convinced that God was real that he changed his name to Paul and spent the rest of his life as a Christian activist. In fact, he became so famous that on his trip to Athens, the intellectual elite of that sophisticated city invited him to speak to the philosophical leaders at the renowned amphitheater on Mars Hill (next to the Acropolis). During his discourse, Paul told these men that they were looking for spiritual satisfaction in all the wrong places. The evidence for God was all around them—even in their own humanity.

> Forasmuch then as we are the offspring of God, we ought not to
> think that the Godhead is like unto gold, or silver, or stone, graven
> by art and man's device. (Acts 17:29)

Scientific interpretation: since we are here, the cause for humanity must be greater than, but similar to, us. Since the dawn of time, it has been observed that people only come from people.

Everything Has a Cause

In ordinary experience, one knows intuitively that nothing happens in isolation. Every event can be traced to one or more events that preceded it and, in fact, caused it. We ask casually: "How did this happen?" or "What caused this?" or "Where did this come from?" Sometimes we try to get at the beginning cause (or first cause) by asking the question: "When did it start?" or more incisively, "Why did this happen?"

When we try to trace an event to its cause, or causes, we find that we never seem to reach a stopping point. The cause of the event was itself caused by a prior cause, which was affected by a previous cause, and so on.

Police investigators at an accident scene, for instance, use the principles of cause and effect to determine who was ultimately responsible and how it happened.

Eventually, we must face the question of the original cause—an uncaused First Cause.

A scientific experiment specifically tries to relate effects to causes in the form of quantitative equations, if possible. Thus, if one repeats the same experiment with exactly the same factors, then exactly the same results will be produced. The very basis of the highly reputed "scientific method" is this very law of causality— that effects are in and like their causes, and that like causes produce like effects. Science in the modern sense would be altogether impossible if cause and effect should cease. This law inevitably leads to a choice between two alternatives: (1) an infinite chain of non-primary causes (nothing is ultimately responsible for all observable causes and effects), or (2) an uncaused primary Cause of all causes (the one absolute Cause that initiated everything).

The Effect Problem

Rationally, it can be concluded that all things began with a single uncaused

First Cause: the God who is above all and existed before all other causes.

The first "universal law" demonstrates the existence of an "uncaused source" or a First Cause by which observable effects came about. But there are also two more related universal laws that we see demonstrated in everything we examine in the world around us. There is no new mass/energy coming into existence anywhere in the universe, and every bit of the original mass/energy is still here. Every time something happens (i.e., an event takes place), some of that energy becomes unavailable.

The First Law of Thermodynamics tells us that matter (mass/energy) can be changed, but can neither be created nor destroyed. The Second Law tells us that all phenomena (mass/energy organized into an "effect") continually proceed to lower levels of usefulness. In simple terms, every cause must be at least as great as the effect that it produces, and will, in reality, produce an effect that is less than the cause. That is, any effect must have a greater cause.

When this universal law is traced backwards, one is faced again with the possibility that there is an ongoing chain of ever-decreasing effects, resulting from an infinite chain of non-primary, ever-increasing causes. However, what appears more probable is the existence of an uncaused and ultimate Source—an omnipotent, omniscient, eternal, and primary First Cause.

The Logical Implications

Applying these principles of cause and effect, it is clear that scientific logic indicates that the Cause for the universe in which we live must trace back to an infinite First Cause of all things. Random motion or primeval particles cannot produce intelligent thought, nor can inert molecules generate spiritual worship.

- The First Cause of limitless space must be infinite.
- The First Cause of endless time must be eternal.
- The First Cause of boundless energy must be omnipotent.
- The First Cause of universal interrelationships must be omnipresent.
- The First Cause of infinite complexity must be omniscient.
- The First Cause of spiritual values must be spiritual.
- The First Cause of human responsibility must be volitional.
- The First Cause of human integrity must be truthful.
- The First Cause of human love must be loving.
- The First Cause of life must be living.

We would conclude from the law of cause and effect that this First Cause of all things must be an infinite, eternal, omnipotent, omnipresent, omniscient, spiritual, volitional, truthful, loving, living Being!

THE TRIUNE UNIVERSE

There is an immeasurably and unimaginably huge universe out there (even though the most important part of it appears to be here). The physical universe is "temporal"—its physical characteristics are defined qualitatively and quantitatively in and by space, time, and mass/energy (usually abbreviated as "matter").

Any effort to determine the cause of the universe is purely hypothetical. No human was there to observe the processes, so any attempt to understand events of prehistory (especially original events) must, therefore, be based on a "belief system," rooted in certain presuppositions. While the theories and ideas may be many, the presuppositions can only be of two sorts: (1) there is an infinite series of causes, going back into infinite time, with no ultimate Cause, or (2) there exists an uncaused First Cause that was external or transcendent to the universe.

Describing the nature of the universe by means of a finite mind and very limited life experience is a bit subjective, to say the least. Apart from information that would have been observed at the time by an intelligent being, the interpretation of the data that we can now glean from our various telescopes or microscopes (as sophisticated as we may believe they are) is really nothing more than complex speculation.

The universe contains "speech" and "knowledge" from the hand of the Creator Himself. Mankind would do well to read His "book."

Time, Space, and Matter

Many scientists today conduct their research based on their presupposition or belief that nothing exists beyond the natural world—that which can be observed around us—and thus they do not accept that any ultimate Cause exists.

Scientists at ICR hold to the presupposition that the uncaused First Cause is the Creator who exists outside of the physical creation He made. Time is not eternal, but created. To ask what happened in time before time was created is to create a meaningless false paradox. There was no "before" prior to the creation of the triune universe of time, space, and mass/energy.

Yet even more amazing (and the universe is amazing) is the historic fact that this Creator-God, after purposefully creating the space-time-matter universe, chose to enter it in the God-human person of Jesus Christ for the sole purpose of providing the means by which humanity could have a personal relationship with the Creator.

> And the Word was made flesh, and dwelt among us, (and we beheld his glory, the glory as of the only begotten of the Father,) full of grace and truth. (John 1:14)

The Triune Godhead

> For this cause I bow my knees unto the Father of our Lord Jesus
> Christ, of whom the whole family in heaven and earth is named,
> that he would grant you, according to the riches of his glory, to
> be strengthened with might by his Spirit in the inner man; that
> Christ may dwell in your hearts by faith; that ye, being rooted and
> grounded in love, may be able to comprehend with all saints what is
> the breadth, and length, and depth, and height; and to know the love
> of Christ, which passeth knowledge, that ye might be filled with all
> the fulness of God. (Ephesians 3:14-19)

The above text encapsulates the doctrine of the Trinity in the Bible. This truth, taught in many other passages of the New Testament, is undoubtedly the most distinctive doctrine of the Christian faith. Most religions are either pantheistic (e.g., Buddhism) or polytheistic (e.g., Hinduism). Two other religions are monotheistic (Judaism and Islam), but only Christianity recognizes the Triune God—Father, Son, Holy Spirit—one God in three Persons.

The sacred book of the Muslims—the Koran—regards Jesus as only a prophet, repeatedly denouncing as infidels all those who believe in the Trinity. The Jews often consider Jesus to have been a great teacher, but no more than that. To the Christian, however, the Lord Jesus Christ is a person, yet God incarnate, God's only begotten Son—Creator, Savior, King of kings and Lord of lords. Christians also believe that the Holy Spirit is not just a spiritual influence, but a real person, the third Person of the Godhead.

God is the infinite, invisible, omnipresent Father, but He is also the Son who is visible, touchable, yet the perfectly holy Word who is always revealing and manifesting the Father, and He is also the Holy Spirit, always present to guide, convict, and comfort. He is the very real, eternal, and invisible, omnipresent Father of all, yet visible and approachable by the Son and experienced and understood through the Holy Spirit. A majestic mystery, but a wonderful reality! Three divine Persons, each equally and totally God.

We cannot adequately comprehend this reality with our finite minds, but we are compelled to acknowledge it and believe it and rejoice with our hearts. And this reality of God's triune nature is somewhat analogous to the "space" of God's created universe. Space is comprised of three dimensions, each of which permeates all space. This structure is helpful to illustrate the nature of the triune God, that God is one God, not three gods, yet revealed as three Persons, each of which is eternally and completely God.

The apostle Peter also noted the action of every Person of the divine Godhead in the great work of saving those who trust in Christ: "Elect according to the foreknowledge of God the Father, through sanctification of the Spirit, unto obedience and sprinkling of the blood of Jesus Christ" (1 Peter 1:2).

It seems that God Himself has made such a model. "For the invisible things of him from the creation of the world are clearly seen, being understood by the things that are made, even his eternal power and Godhead" (Romans 1:20). That is, the creation itself can be seen as a model of the three-in-one Godhead.

Space, both invisible and at the same time the matrix in which all of our reality exists, is analogous to the heavenly Father. "No man hath seen God at any time" (1 John 4:12). "In him we live, and move, and have our being" (Acts 17:28).

Matter (mass/energy) is the visible and tangible revelation of the existence of space. We "see" space by means of the visible phenomena present in Jesus. Just so, God the Son is the "Word" (John 1:14) that makes it possible for us to "see" God. "He that hath seen me hath seen the Father" (John 14:9). Jesus Christ is the "fullness of the Godhead bodily" (Colossians 2:9).

Time is the means by which we experience our reality. Matter is really mass/energy operating in a very specific way through time. Were there no time, nothing would function—nothing would "happen." And that "event fulfillment" is the ministry of the Holy Spirit. He is the One who causes us to be "born again" (1 Corinthians 6:11). He is the One who imparts the spiritual gifts of God to the believers (1 Corinthians 12:8). Indeed, the Holy Spirit is the One who "guides" into truth (John 16:13) and brings conviction about the need for truth (John 16:8).

The only accurate illustration of the triune God is given by the Creator Himself by the "things that are made."

THE TRIUNE GOD

Manifested by and analogous to His creation

Father = SPACE	Son = MATTER	Spirit = TIME
Invisible	Visible	Sensed & Felt
Omnipresent	Tangible	Understood
Source	Present Reality	Future
God Framed	God Manifested	God Experienced
Authority	Declaration	Appropriation

Deuteronomy 6:4

The physical universe is, in a very real sense, a trinity of trinities. Also, in a certain sense, human life is a trinity of body, soul, and spirit. In fact, tri-unity in various ways is often seen in the creation. (However, note that a "trinity" is not an entity composed of three individual parts, like the sides of a triangle, but rather an entity of three parts, each of which is the whole.)

Although no man could ever model the Godhead, God has seemingly done this in His creation. The third mention of the Godhead is given in Colossians 2:9. "For in [Christ] dwelleth all the fulness of the Godhead bodily." Thus, the Lord Jesus can say to His disciples: "He that hath seen me hath seen the Father" (John 14:9), for He Himself is "the image of the invisible God" (Colossians 1:15).

DESIGN AND PURPOSE

Human beings are unique from every other living organism in the world, specially created and specially purposed. The earth is also like no other planet, specially created by God for humans, and we can easily observe evidence of His design in His creation.

Beauty

Aesthetics is the study of beauty, more often associated today with art. However, the discipline itself and the philosophical apologetics from the concept are extended into every sphere of imagination, sensibility, and taste. God saw that His creation was good, in appearance as well as in all other sensory aspects, and humans get to "behold" beauty because He first caused beauty to exist.

Essentially, the foundational argument would suggest that given the universal reality that the concept of beauty exists (even if it is "in the eye of the beholder"), there is an ultimate standard by which beauty is judged. Determining the aesthetic value of anything requires rational judgment, even though that judgment is unique to each individual. Each rational judgment must rely on one's ability to discriminate at a sensory or emotional level.

This examination makes a judgment regarding whether something is beautiful, sublime, disgusting, fun, cute, silly, entertaining, pretentious, discordant, harmonious, boring, humorous, or tragic. And, of course, since such ability exists only in the mental acuity of imaginative appreciation, then the Source of such ability must also be both rational and emotional.

The vast differences between individual tastes and even between cultures, both in time and in location, speak to the enormity of such possibilities and to the unfathomable wonder of the hunger for beauty in every human being.

That such a hunger exists only in human beings is a wonder in itself! The flower is not impressed with its own majesty; it merely exists with no conscious awareness. The chimpanzee does not gaze longingly on the enigma of the *Mona Lisa*, nor do the stars muse on the heavens they themselves grace.

In fact, all humanity eschews destruction and random chaos as "ugly" and attempts to mask death with various levels of cosmetic disguises, which speaks to the realization that some sights and sounds are not beautiful, and thus there must exist a standard of "perfect" beauty.

Justice

Our postmodern age has redefined "right" and "wrong" in terms of subjective feelings and personal perspectives. Yet despite the passing of the ages, humans still have an innate sense of absolute right and wrong. Why? Because God Himself is just.

Morality involves the study of the universal recognition that "good" is better than "evil," which logically requires the existence of an ultimate Judge. That is, since all humanity accepts the knowledge that certain events and standards are better than others, even though cultures may differ on what those events or standards may be, there must be an ultimate Source of such thinking, even if the absolute standard has become distorted over time.

C.S. Lewis, one of the most prolific writers and thinkers of our time, wrote of what he called Moral Law, or the Law of Human Nature, in his work *Mere Christianity*.

> The Moral Law, or Law of Human Nature, is not simply a fact about human behaviour in the same way as the Law of Gravitation is, or may be, simply a fact about how heavy objects behave. On the other hand, it is not a mere fancy, for we cannot get rid of the idea, and most of the things we say and think about men would be reduced to nonsense if we did. And it is not simply a statement about how we should like men to behave for our own convenience; for the behaviour we call bad or unfair is not exactly the same as the behaviour we find inconvenient, and may even be the opposite. Consequently, the Rule of Right and Wrong, or Law of Human Nature, or whatever you call it, must somehow or other be a real thing—a thing that is really there, not made up by ourselves.[1]

We find then that we do not exist on our own, that we are under a law, and that Somebody or Something wants us to behave in a certain way.

Therefore, this Somebody or Something is directing the universe, and as a result we sense an internal law that urges us to do right and makes us feel responsible and even uncomfortable when we do wrong. We have to assume this entity is more like a mind than it is like anything else we know, because after all, the only

---

1. Lewis, C. S. 1952. *Mere Christianity*. New York: Macmillan Publishing, 30.

other thing we know is matter and you can hardly imagine a bit of matter giving instructions.

Catholic apologist and philosophy professor Peter Kreeft writes in his work *The Argument from Conscience:* "The only possible source of absolute authority is an absolute perfect will."[2]

Love

Like gravity and aerodynamics, we cannot scientifically prove the existence of love, yet we know it exists and can observe its effects. Unlike affection, only humans are capable of receiving, giving, refusing, and rejecting love.

Animals (including chimps) are not able to provide any assistance to other creatures they are not related to, and even seem to be unable to recognize the needs of other animals. Although some animals (especially mammals like dogs, cats, and horses) can and do appreciate affection, only humans are capable of love.

Humans are driven by an entirely different kind of emotion. We love our children when they are disobedient. We can love our enemies and sacrifice our lives for our friends (like soldiers do). The highest, truest kind of love is that which consciously seeks and takes practical action to do good for someone else, valuing that other person higher than one's self, even if providing such good requires self-sacrifice. This is what separates us, practically, from the "love" expressed by animals.

Of course, if God did not create us, how would we ever know what real love is, much less learn to practice love ourselves? The very fact that we can love and be loved (by God and by others) is yet another proof of a Creator's love. Because of His own nature of infinite love and grace, it was God's good pleasure to create beings on whom He could bestow His love and grace and who, being made in His image, would be capable of reciprocating and responding to that love. "But God commendeth his love toward us, in that, while we were yet sinners, Christ died for us" (Romans 5:8).

Meaning

Humans, in particular, seek a "reason to exist" and for the most part find it difficult to accept that we are simply here to consume the earth's resources and die. However, in the beginning God created the heavens, the earth, and all living creatures—especially mankind—with special purposes in mind, which He explained in His Word. Every part of creation has a specific meaning and purpose for existing, which we can most easily observe in the study of various ecosystems.

---

2.   The full text of *Argument* can be viewed at http://www.peterkreeft.com/topics/conscience.htm.

In contrast, here is the essence of the naturalistic-evolutionary "story."

There is no God (or "god" is in the forces of nature, or in man himself). Nothing "supernatural" exists (except perhaps some "extra-terrestrial" race of super-intellects that have evolved in other parts of the universe). Since no evidence exists for the God of the Bible, we can be certain that there is no such thing as a "plan for your life." Thus, there is no future, no "afterlife." Speculative Hollywood movies notwithstanding, and the many reported "out of the body experiences" to the contrary, no rational naturalist believes in any form of "eternal life." When you're dead, you're dead!

Such hopeless beliefs drive many into lives of debauchery and hedonism, and fill the couches of psychologists and psychiatrists all over the world. Teenage suicide is alarmingly high, and the therapists themselves continue to manifest one of the highest suicide rates in civilized countries. Scandals abound among the leaders of world business, politics, and churches.

> If in this life only we have hope in Christ, we are of all men most miserable. (1 Corinthians 15:19)

There is no "good news" in the evolutionary theory.

There is, however, glorious wonder and life-changing power in the "everlasting gospel" (Revelation 14:6). There is:

- power to transform (Romans 12:2)
- power to enrich (2 Corinthians 9:11)
- power to bring satisfying peace to all situations (Hebrews 13:20-21)
- power to change the mortal body into the immortal and everlasting being that will live eternally with the Creator (1 Corinthians 15:53-54)

Conventional wisdom says to "grab all the gusto you can; you only go around once in life!" We are told to "just be yourself" and that we should "let the good times roll." These and hundreds more clichés sprinkled throughout our culture misdirect our thinking and undermine real satisfaction, purpose, and meaning in life.

God designed humanity to enjoy the happiness of stability, the happiness of productivity, and the happiness of success (see Psalm 1). Jesus said, "I am come that they might have life, and that they might have it more abundantly" (John 10:10).

Order

Ordered systems or structures do not happen spontaneously. We never observe orderliness occurring by accident, without an intelligent cause to direct the order. No amount of undirected power or energy is enough to bring order out of chaos. Try shooting a wristwatch with a bullet; the watch's order does not increase! (The only order in a watch is that which the watchmaker intelligently puts into it at the beginning.)

Likewise, if we drop a plain glass bottle of spoiled milk onto bricks, it quite naturally shatters into a more disorderly arrangement: chaotic glass fragments mixed with spilt spoiled milk. It could never reform itself into a more exquisitely-sculpted glass container containing fresh milk!

The addition of huge amounts of energy is not enough, either. A tired human eats to gain food energy, but eating hot coals is not an adequate energy source, because it fails to match and cooperate with the orderly design of human digestive systems.

Everyday experiences, such as broken watches and spilled milk, remind us that order does not happen by itself. In fact, our entire universe demonstrates that same truth. The earth's rotation, the moon cycle, and the changing seasons are just a few of the ordered processes observable in nature. These processes don't happen randomly but rather are divinely caused by God.

God is the Author and Organizer of orderliness. His design and construction of our own bodies, through the complexity of biogenesis, is a proper reason for glorifying and thanking Him for making us. As wild and untamed as our world is, everything in nature follows a specific order orchestrated by God.

Wisdom

All organisms react to their environments, but human beings are the only creatures capable of rationalization and acquiring knowledge and wisdom. That is because humans are the only part of the universe that was made in the Creator's "image."

Wisdom is, essentially, the effective understanding and use of information. Humans discover information; we do not invent it. Through wisdom, humanity has developed (i.e., used information effectively) a set of scientific laws that elegantly expresses reality in the language of mathematics. Johann Kepler, the noted founder of physical astronomy, is said to have considered his science to be "thinking God's thoughts after Him."

The unfathomable intelligence that was used to invent the universe, and to pre-program its interactive workings, is a source of "wisdom" beyond any imagination. In particular, the cause of our universe coming into being, and of its continuing to operate as it does, is a dynamic display of the Creator's wisdom, some of which we can scientifically understand and effectively apply. When we do, we are "thinking God's thoughts after Him."

To the extent that humans have any wisdom at all, much less the wisdom necessary to understand a meaningful amount of the workings of the universe, the very fact that we can understand at all is more amazing than the marvelous physics of the universe! How can an immaterial mind, residing inside a human body, made mostly of water (along with other constituent elements of the earth), comprehend anything—even this sentence?

It is only by God's creative grace that human beings can think any thoughts at all, much less thoughts that are logical and analytical enough to be called "scientific."

FOR FURTHER STUDY

The articles listed below are available at www.icr.org. Find the "Search" bar on the opening page of the website, type in the title of the article that you wish to read, and click "Enter." The web search will take you directly to the article.

Did God Create the Earth in Its Present Conditions?

Did the Watchmaker Make the Watch?

For Every Structure There Is a Reason

Glory and Thanks

Some Recent Developments Having to Do with Time

The Cosmic Bubbleland

The Creator in His Word: Does Genesis Address the Time of Creation, or Just the Fact…?

The Foolishness of Human Wisdom

The Mathematical Impossibility of Evolution

The Plasma Universe

The Tri-Universe

The Wisdom Mine

Thinking God's Thoughts after Him

What Makes Us Human?

Where Did Love Come From?

Where Is Wisdom?

Why Did God Create Us?

EVIDENCE

for

TRUTH

*Buy the truth, and sell it not; also wisdom,
and instruction, and understanding.*

Proverbs 23:23

EVIDENCE
for
TRUTH

Roman Governor Pontius Pilate's famous question "What is truth?" (John 18:38) is answered in absolute terms by Jesus Christ: "And ye shall know the truth, and the truth shall make you free" (John 8:32). If truth is knowable, then it should follow that there would be ample evidence of truth in and around our universe. While we each have unique, subjective experiences, there is an absolute, objective truth that is obvious to everyone.

NATURAL LAWS

Inescapable laws in nature exist for our benefit, our advantage, and our protection. We can observe these laws in action all around us.

Science Is Founded on Absolute Truth

Scientific knowledge requires an absolute standard of truth that can be discovered. Scientific knowledge is not a collection of subjective opinions. Rather, it is a collection of explanations about objective reality that is based on observed or predicted phenomena. In addition, these explanations must be verified repeatedly to confirm that they correctly model reality.

As our technical ability to observe reality improves, we are able to increase the quality and quantity of our observations. Better-observed data challenge our explanations, some of which will no longer fit the observed facts. New theories are then formed and either verified or falsified.

While our scientific knowledge changes rapidly, the absolute reality being modeled has never changed. The scientific method assumes an absolute reality against which theories can be verified.

Science Tests Subjective Experience Against Absolute Truth

The scientific method compares our limited understanding with the absolute truth of reality.

Empirical Science Is Based on Observation

The scientific method requires that the scientist test a theory based on observed or predicted facts. The scientist must formulate a theory or hypothesis based on what has been observed, then design a test by which the theory may be verified as valid or not.

If the theory produces observed events that correspond with the theory postulated in advance, then the scientist has a serious beginning point from which to claim further science (knowledge) about the specific test.

Over the last several hundred years, a number of theories have been repeated so often that they are now considered "scientific laws." Scientists are confident that these laws correctly model the absolute truth of reality.

Should someone claim they have had a subjective experience that contradicts one of these laws, the burden of proof is on that person to prove that they can repeatedly demonstrate that the law is false. The standard of measure remains absolute truth about reality, verified through repeated observation.

Historical Science Is Based on Assumptions

Scientists observe actual events. Past events are different from events that are repeatable and observable. The scientific method is limited to that which can be tested, reproduced, and falsified. That which lies outside of these parameters is not science but is in the realm of faith, the untestable assumptions based on the presumption of naturalism or the revelation of creation.

Science can test an assumption by evaluating the accuracy of the predictions of the different models. That model (theory, belief, revelation) that best predicts that which is observable is the more creditable model of reality. However, since new observations cannot be made about past events, verification is limited.

The assumptions the scientist brings to the study of origins can obscure the evidence. Historical science does not benefit from the repeatable observations that have served as the cauldron of truth for scientific knowledge.

The Laws of Science Require a Creator

The universe has been created with very special scientific laws that enable us to both live and learn of them. The laws of nature do not have a naturalistic cause. The cause of the laws of nature was not the laws of nature.

> The miracle of the appropriateness of the language of mathematics for the formulation of the laws of physics is a wonderful gift which we neither understand nor deserve.[3] (Eugene P. Wigner)

There is an objective mathematical structure seen in the physical universe. An example is the relationship of the periodic table and mathematics. One element is distinguished from another by the number of electrons, neutrons, and protons.

---

3.   Wigner, E.P. 1960. The Unreasonable Effectiveness of Mathematics in the Natural Sciences. *Communications in Pure and Applied Mathematics,* vol. 13, No. I. New York: John Wiley & Sons, Inc.

How can it be that mathematics, being after all a product of human thought which is independent of experience, is so admirably appropriate to the objects of reality?[4] (Albert Einstein)

HUMAN CONSCIENCE

Regardless of cultural norms, humans all over the world have an innate sense of good and evil that demonstrates God's design in us. Everyone is given a sense of morality. We were created to love our Creator and to love one another. We experience guilt when we do not.

All Men Know That Good Is Better Than Evil

All societies try, or claim to try, to suppress "evil" and promote "good." Kindness and care for family members, especially for children, are universal traits. Compassion for the elderly, poor, and weak are qualities valued by cultures around the world. Instead of "might makes right," our consciences teach us that might should choose to do right. This reflects our God-given command to care for each other.

A naturalistic model of origins would not predict socially-established actions like care and kindness, actions that every culture recognizes as "good." Selfish and cruel use of force—"survival of the fittest"—is routinely condemned, not praised.

All Men Acknowledge a Spiritual Part of Life

All societies are permeated with "religious" worship and/or sensitivity to "spiritual" things. Somehow what is "spiritual" is connected to what we call our conscience. While every culture differs, each one displays an interest in knowing and honoring God, or else a religious disposition to try to substitute someone or something in God's place.

There is a universal desire to know and be known by God, or by a substitute for Him. Likewise, there is a worldwide hunger to be rescued from moral failures and misbehaviors, as well as a serious concern for what happens after we die.

All Men Recognize Human Authority over Earth and Its Animals

All societies demonstrate and understand that humans dominate the earth, ruling over animals, plant life, and the physical environment. All cultures have acknowledged the superiority of man over all other animate life, life forms, and inanimate objects in nature, as reflected in the Dominion Mandate assigned to mankind by God (Genesis 1:28).

---

4. Einstein, A. 1983. *Sidelights on Relativity*. New York: Dover.

Man's authority over animals, plants, and the rest of the earth has changed history through the use and consumption of animals (livestock, riding horses, fishing, etc.) and plants (timber for wood, crops for food, etc.), as well as the physical environment (diverting river water for irrigation, harnessing wind power for sailing and windmills, using rocks for buildings, etc.).

In addition, all societies have a spoken language of abstract thought and concepts. Human communication is very different from anything observed in animals. Why? Mankind knows he is the proper creature fit to rule the earth. This makes sense only if man was created to be morally superior to animals, plants, and the earth.

DESIRE FOR JUSTICE

Humans in general, despite our cultural upbringings, have a natural dislike for injustice and a natural desire to see justice served.

The universal desire for "equal justice" (and "just laws") is a demonstration of mankind's moral nature, which can only be adequately explained by man (both male and female) being a unique creature, created in God's image. Evolution would postulate that man is different from "other" animals only in degree, not kind. Mankind's innate desire for justice is a proof of mankind's inherently moral nature, which itself is a proof of God's status as Creator.

Equal Justice Requires Universal Laws

Real justice is "equal." Equal justice requires universal laws. But universal laws do not emerge randomly; they need a universal Lawgiver. As a matter of moral justice, crimes and other types of social wrongdoing require a just consequence.

Although the details of each wrongdoing vary and should be balanced and weighed against relevant circumstances, real justice is ultimately "equal" to the offense committed (or else it is not truly just). Yet "equal" justice, whether penal or compensatory, requires universal laws in order to achieve equality in application.

Universal laws don't emerge randomly or by accident. Universal laws—and equal justice—must come from a universal and just Lawgiver, God Himself.

When our desire for equal justice through the application of universal laws is frustrated, this frustration is an indication of our sense that there is a Lawgiver (and Judge) above and beyond our society and culture (as well as all others). People throughout history have held the expectation that they will be judged after death. The timeless practice of recognizing injustices in this life, and expecting all injustices to be resolved hereafter by a truly equal justice, reveals an intuitive sense that God's universal justice, some day, will be meted out according to His universal laws.

Just Laws Rely on Truth

Laws based on falsehood or wrong are not just laws. Just laws must be based on what is true and what is right. Societies need to apply just laws in order to resolve social disputes and problems; personal rights, valuable relationships, and social responsibilities are at stake. Therefore, the legal system needs to recognize and uphold the true and the right, while rejecting the false and the wrong.

But to have just laws enforced, truth must be distinguishable from falsehood, and right from wrong. Does such a law exist?

One objective moral standard is the justice principle called the Golden Rule: the standard of evaluating our own actions as just or unjust based on whether we would want those same actions to be done to us. This is a type of universal law that is "written in [our] hearts" (Romans 2:15). Slanderers don't think it right when they themselves are slandered. Likewise, thieves don't feel right about their own property being stolen. Even savage cannibals don't want to be eaten by their neighbors!

Reliable Evidence Is Required

To have justice, we need just laws. But just laws cannot work apart from true evidence, which is necessary for us to recognize what is relevant and true. Analyzing evidence requires recognizing relevance and testing for truth. Just laws rely on truth and right. But to recognize truth and right, we need reliable evidence to show what is true and right. (Sometimes this can be meaningfully corroborated by disproving something as false or wrong.)

The idea of an orderly process for scrutinizing and testing something offered as "evidence," when properly submitted for examination (and cross-examination), underlies the logic of the Rules of Evidence that we use in our court systems.

Over the past centuries, the search for truth in science has been formalized into the process known as the *scientific method*, whereby theories are developed and tested according to a generally-accepted standard. In a similar fashion, the legal profession operates by what is known as the Rules of Evidence.

The focus of the Federal Rules of Evidence is evidentiary reliability. Why? Because just laws need reliable evidence. Whether that evidence is forensic evidence, empirical evidence, or a combination of both, the fundamental issue is, or at least should be, recognizing truth.

FOR FURTHER STUDY

The articles listed below are available at www.icr.org. Find the "Search" bar on the opening page of the website, type in the title of the article that you wish to read, and click "Enter." The web search will take you directly to the article.

What Makes Us Human?

Adam and the Animals

Can Research Be Done from a Creation Base?

Creation and the Environment

Exploring the Limitations of the Scientific Method

Has the Missing Link Been Found?

Inspired Guesses, Creative Imagination, and Science

Is Man a "Higher Animal"?

Language, Creation and the Inner Man

Maker and Owner

The Evidence of Nothing

The Golden Rule

The Pursuit of Happiness

The Splendid Faith of the Evolutionist

The Witness of Conscience

Why Do We Marry?

Are All Men Created Equal?

EVIDENCE *from* NATURE

The heavens declare the glory of God; and the firmament sheweth his handywork. Day unto day uttereth speech, and night unto night sheweth knowledge.

Psalm 19:1-2

EVIDENCE *from* NATURE

NATURE IS GOD'S "LANGUAGE" FOR ALL HUMANITY

The evidence for creation can be clearly seen from that which has been made by our Creator. Our planet has been uniquely created by God for life, especially human life. Our universe is filled with wonder that demonstrates our wonderful Creator. Through what was made we can see God's power, presence, protection, provision, and wisdom. Nature eloquently testifies to an infinite, eternal, omnipotent, omniscient, living, personal God.

Nature Reveals God's Power

The awesome power of our Creator is seen throughout the universe. Even a child can see stars at night. But who has the power necessary to put them there?

A small reflection of the power of our Creator is seen in the thousands of stars that shine in the night sky. Galaxies consist of millions of stars packed close together. And billions of galaxies fill the universe. The amount of power displayed in the heavens is overwhelming, if we take the time to look up at night and think about it. This reveals God's power at the cosmic level.

Everyone can appreciate sun-power. The sun lights our days so we can see nature all around us. (Even a blind person can feel the warmth of the sun.) Our sun and other stars are bright because they radiate energy, both visible and invisible. Some of this energy radiating from the sun is needed, directly or indirectly, to power all life forms on earth. Some of the other energy, also very powerful, is harmful to life.

The energy that is useful to life is a very small part of the spectrum. That part is also the part that we can see. Due to the laws of physics established by our Creator, visible light is the best energy for the chemical reactions of life. Unlike high-energy radiation, such as x-rays and gamma rays (which harm living cells), visible light enables human eyes to see, plus it powers plant growth, the foundation of all food chains on earth. Even the energetic behavior of little bugs ultimately depends on sun-power.

God's power extends from wonders great and small that we can observe in our awesome universe, like the sun and stars (which look small to us, yet are huge in actual size).

The study of "power" is called thermodynamics. That term is a compound of two Greek words, *therme* ("heat") and *dunamis* ("power"). It is the science that speaks of the power or energy contained in heat, and its conversion to other forms of energy. The term "energy" is itself derived from the Greek word *energeia* ("working"), and is normally defined as "the capacity to do work." In modern scientific terminology, "energy" and "work" are considered equivalent. Something which has "energy" has the "capacity to do work"—that is, the capacity to exert a force through a distance.

The concept of "power" is closely related to that of "energy." Power is the work done, or the energy expended to do the work, per unit of time measured in foot-pounds per second.

Since all processes are fundamentally energy conversion processes, and since everything that happens in the physical universe is a "process" of some kind, it is obvious why the study of thermodynamics is recognized as the most universal and fundamental of all science. Everything that exists in the universe is some form of energy, and everything that happens is some form of energy conversion.

The reason why no energy can now be created is because only God can create energy and because God has "rested from all his work which God created and made" (Genesis 2:3). The reason why energy cannot now be destroyed is because He is now "upholding all things by the word of his power" (Hebrews 1:3).

"I know that, whatsoever God doeth, it shall be forever: nothing can be put to it, nor any thing taken from it" (Ecclesiastes 3:14).

Nature Reveals God's Presence

The presence of God is evident everywhere, in the immensity of the universe, and at levels so small the human eye cannot see. The Bible teaches that the universe is as infinitely great as the very thoughts and ways of God (Isaiah 55:9), and that it will endure forever (Ecclesiastes 3:14; Psalm 148:1-6; Daniel 12:3). We can study it and describe it and serve in it eternally without ever exhausting its infinite beauties and mysteries.

God's presence can be detected even in the most commonplace substances, like water. All of us have physical bodies that are mostly water! God provides the water for life. Our planet is close enough to the sun to provide the liquid water that is necessary for life. But if it were just a little farther away, all that water would become ice!

While water itself is a very small molecule (just a 3-atom unit of hydrogen and oxygen), it is the primary ingredient of our planet (i.e., earth's "biggest" component). God's design of how water's specific molecules behave (and the impact water has on our entire planet) is an example of God's creative design and custodial presence, even on the smallest and largest scales.

Water expands when it freezes, unlike most other substances. Ice and snow take up more volume than the same amount of liquid water. This makes water denser as a liquid than it is when frozen, so ice floats. If ice did not float on the surface of water, the floors of the oceans and lakes would be covered with glaciers of ice that would never melt. Surface ice also helps regulate the climate by reflecting energy.

As a liquid, water's temperature range is perfect for cycling water from the oceans to the land. Water requires a lot of energy to evaporate into a vapor, and it releases this energy when it condenses back into liquid. This balances temperatures in the earth's climate, as well as inside living cells. If less energy were required for evaporation, then streams, rivers, and lakes would evaporate away quickly.

Beautiful clouds and sunsets inspire praise for the Creator who forms them. Because God's creative presence is shown in even commonplace yet needful things, we are blessed by the huge quantities of water that flow though our biosphere.

Nature Reveals God's Protection

Life itself is fragile, yet the protection of life can be seen in the careful design of our physical environment. Our bodies need many forms of protection, from exotic dangers, such as rocks falling from space, to the mundane, such as temperature control.

If our earth had a thinner atmosphere, our planet would be hit with lethal amounts of incoming rocks and harmful radiation. Mercury, Pluto, and the moon have almost no air at all. Their surfaces are scarred with craters from the impacts of giant boulders, little pebbles, and small grains of sand. The surfaces of these planets are very hot when facing the sun, and very cold when facing away. If earth had a thicker atmosphere, our planet would be boiling hot. The weight of the atmosphere on Venus and the "gas giant" planets (Jupiter, Saturn, Uranus, and Neptune) is very heavy. On Venus, for instance, the surface pressure is 90 times that of earth! The surface pressures of Jupiter, Saturn, Uranus, and Neptune are even higher.

Earth has just the right mixture of nitrogen and oxygen in its atmosphere. Venus and the gas giants have the wrong kind of gases for humans (or any other life forms) to survive there. Venus is mostly carbon dioxide. The gas giants are mostly hydrogen and helium. The other planets have little or no "air" at all. Truly, the very air we breathe is an invisible yet universal witness to God's protective providence.

Sunlight reaches us through our transparent atmosphere. Even though we can see through it, our atmosphere is also a filter. It allows in the sun's radiation that is useful to life, but mostly blocks the radiation that is harmful to life. Only a fraction of the radio waves and some of the visible light and infrared radiations are blocked, but almost all of the harmful ultraviolet rays, x-rays, and gamma rays never reach us.

We have been given an atmosphere that protects us. It provides just the right amount of air and warmth we need. It allows the sunlight to reach the plants that feed us. Our transparent atmosphere not only protects us, but it allows us to the see the stars and wonders of the heavens. The question is: Are these marvelous devices merely accidents, or are they evidence of incredible design by a Creator?

Design in living things is obvious. Even a single-celled organism is complex beyond the ability of scientists to understand, let alone duplicate. All of life is governed by the marvelously complex genetic code, which contains not only design and order, but what is equivalent to written information. This DNA code must not only be written correctly, the rest of the cell must be able to read it and follow its instructions if the cell is to metabolize its food, carry out the myriad of enzyme reactions, and, especially, to reproduce. This code had to be present at the origin of life.

The human eye is an obvious example of design. With its many functioning parts—the lens, cornea, iris, the controlling muscles, the sensitive rods and cones which translate light energy into chemical signals, the optic nerve which speeds these signals to a decoding center in the brain, and on and on—the eye was unquestionably designed by an incredibly intelligent Designer who had a complete grasp of optical physics.

The list is endless. God has provided overwhelming evidence of His care in the design of our universe, our earth, all living things—but especially humans. Everywhere and everything bears the fingerprints of an omniscient Designer who loves and cares for His creation.

Nature Reveals God's Provision

The provision of every good thing in nature that is needful or useful for humans or other creatures comes from our Creator. God provides everything we need. Consider this: Why does the earth provide edible food in the first place? If the planting and harvesting of crops were not so commonplace, we would (or should) regard the growing cycles of corn, beans, fruit trees, potatoes, or any other plant as amazing miracles.

The sun's energy warms our planet. Hot air blows from areas heated by the sun to cooler areas. The sun's energy brings rain. Water evaporates from the ocean and falls to the land as it cools. The sun powers the winds that move the water vapor to the land. The sun's energy renews the air. With our sun's energy, plants convert carbon dioxide into oxygen. The sun's energy grows food. Plants capture sunlight and store it in sugar, starch, and fat.

Many other stars are too hot to support life. Many are too cold. Some vary from hot to cold too much. Some stars are too big and some are too small. Our sun is one of the few ideally suited to support life. It has the right brightness and variability. It radiates the right range of energy in the right amounts. Most stars in the universe are not perfectly balanced for life, but our sun is.

There are thousands of examples of an integrated and purposeful plan for provision throughout the flora and fauna of our planet. Everywhere one looks, if one really tries to understand what is going on, it is easy to see an intelligent Designer behind the common, everyday occurrences of our world.

Bread in one form or another is beyond question the most basic form of food in practically every human society, past or present, so much so that it is often called "the staff of life." Fossilized cakes of bread have even been found in a number of ancient archaeological sites.

That ordinary food, so common throughout the world, has been made from many different kinds of grain. The wheat or barley or other grain is first ground into flour, then mixed with water, then baked into cakes or loaves. Various other ingredients are often added to produce different varieties of bread, but each type of bread almost inevitably becomes the most essential foodstuff of that society.

There was one special time when God's chosen people had to live in a hostile desert environment for forty years and could neither plant grain nor produce bread. In answer to their prayers, however, God "satisfied them with the bread of heaven" (Psalm 105:40). That was the wonderful *manna*, which miraculously appeared on the ground each day there in the wilderness. The manna bread was actually called "the corn of heaven" and "angels' food" (Psalm 78:24-25).

Whether a unique provision like manna or an ordinary provision through the growth of the grain that we take for granted, God provides it all, "for he maketh his sun to rise on the evil and on the good, and sendeth rain on the just and on the unjust" (Matthew 5:45).

Nature Reveals God's Wisdom

The wisdom and cleverness of our Creator is seen in the orderly structure and complexity of life and the systems that demonstrate intelligence while supporting that life. Wisdom enables us to understand reality. Through wisdom we have discovered a set of scientific laws that elegantly express reality in the language of mathematics. Whenever man learns the logic of the universe, man is (in essence) "thinking God's thoughts after Him." A correct "understanding" of understanding, therefore, is that we humans discover (and implement) wisdom; we do not invent it.

In particular, the cause of our universe coming into being, and of its continuing to operate as it does, is a dynamic display of the Creator's wisdom, some of which we can scientifically discover and understand. When we do, it is like walking in the footprints of someone who previously walked through a snowdrift.

The unfathomable amount of applied knowledge (wisdom) that was used to invent the universe, and to pre-program its interactive workings, is a source of wonder beyond the imagination. David the psalmist asked, in light of the stupendous power and quantity displayed in the heavens, "What is man," that God is mindful of him? (Psalm 8:3-4).

How could a creature such as a human begin to comprehend the wisdom built into the interactive universe? To the extent that we humans have any wisdom at all, much less the wisdom necessary to understand a meaningful amount of the universe's workings, our understanding is itself more amazing than the physics of the universe! For how can an immaterial mind, residing inside a human body, a "bone-house" made of water and other constituent elements of the earth, comprehend anything?

As noted in the discussion on cause and effect, it is only by God's creative grace that human creatures like us can think any thoughts at all, much less thoughts that are logical and analytical enough to be called "scientific." Because God's wisdom is displayed in the universe itself, and also in our human ability to comprehend that universe, we owe our great Creator-God an ongoing debt of creaturely thanksgiving.

It must be acknowledged that one cannot prove, scientifically, that the animal or human brain was created by a Supreme Intelligence. The question of origins—creation or evolution—is almost entirely outside the experimental domain of science, for when the first brain was formed, there were no human observers. Cognitively, however, and from observation, it is reasonable to conclude that the human brain was created.

If we choose to believe that we are the product of chance and random processes (evolution), where man is perhaps merely of the highest order, then we will possess a materialistic and relativistic philosophy. On the other hand, if we choose to believe that our brain was created by a Master Intelligence, then we will have a theological worldview, one which should prompt us to use our minds to understand His purpose for His creation.

This was, after all, the conclusion of no less than Johann Kepler, a creationist and arguably the greatest of all scientists, who declared that we had been created "to think God's thoughts after Him."

THE EARTH IS UNIQUE

Secularists like to consider earth as just one of many millions of planets, occupying an obscure place in an insignificant galaxy in a sea of nothingness. The Bible teaches, however, that earth is very special to the Creator, performing a crucial role in the universe today, and prepared for an unending role in the cosmic saga.

Earth is the location God chose to situate His image in man after He had created and constructed it and him in wisdom. This is where God sent His only begotten Son, to live a perfect life and die a sufficient sacrifice once man had rejected Him. It is also special in a temporal sense, well-designed for man's habitation. God created it in an orderly fashion, with each step necessary for the life and well-being of man.

As far as science "knows," planet earth is unique in the entire universe. Certainly this is true in our own solar system. Nothing we have observed leads us to believe that there is any other planet like earth.

The Earth Itself

A brief glance at the earth compared to all other known planets reveals many contrasts. Even from outer space, the earth stands in stark contrast to the other seven planets in our solar system. Earth is the only planet circling our sun on which life as we know it could (and does) exist.

Like no other planet, ours is covered with green vegetation, enormous blue-green oceans containing over a million islands, hundreds of thousands of streams and rivers, huge land masses called continents, mountains, ice caps, and deserts that produce a spectacular variety of color and texture. Some form of life is found in virtually every ecological niche on the earth's surface. Even in the extremely cold Antarctica, hardy microscopic beings thrive in ponds, tiny wingless insects live in patches of moss and lichen, and plants grow and flower yearly. From the apex of the atmosphere to the bottom of the oceans, from the coldest part of the poles to the warmest part of the equator, life thrives here. To this day, no evidence of life has been found on any other planet.

The earth is immense in size, about 8,000 miles in diameter, with a mass calculated at roughly $6.6 \times 1,021$ tons. The earth is on average 93 million miles from the sun. If the earth traveled much faster in its 584-million-mile-long journey around the sun, its orbit would become larger and it would move farther away from the sun. If it moved too far from this narrow habitable zone, all life would cease to exist on earth. If it traveled slightly slower in its orbit, the earth would move closer to the sun, and if it moved too close, all life would likewise perish. The earth's 365-days, 6-hours, 49-minutes, and 9.54-seconds trip around the sun (the sidereal year) is consistent to over a thousandth of a second!

If the yearly average temperature on earth's surface changed by only a few degrees or so, much of the life on it would eventually roast or freeze. This change would upset the water-to-ice ratio and other critical balances, with disastrous results. If the earth rotated slower on its axis, all life would die in time, either by freezing at night because of lack of heat from the sun or by burning during the day from too much heat.

Our "normal" earth processes are assuredly unique among the planets in our solar system and, according to what we know, in the entire universe.

The Sun and Moon

Of all the energy the sun gives off, only 0.45 billionth of its daily output strikes the earth. The sun provides the earth with energy estimated at over 239 trillion horsepower, about 35,000 horsepower for each current resident. Even though there likely exists several hundred billion galaxies in the universe, each with 100 billion stars, there is only one atom for every 88 gallons of space, which means the vast majority of the universe is empty space!

Our sun belongs to a spectral class representing only 5% of all stars: a G2V yellow dwarf main sequence variable. Many in this class pulsate much more radically than the sun, giving off deadly flares. Some flares and coronal mass ejections have topped the charts in recent years. The energy of these magnetic storms escapes between the granules instead of heating the photosphere. As a result, the sun's heat output, or solar constant, has only varied by 6 one-hundredths of a percent during the entire observational period of 1974-2006.

How does our sun compare with its classmates? In one of the longest-running observational programs of the 20th century, researchers White, Wallace, and Livingstone published the results of their "Sun-as-a-Star" program in the *Astrophysical Journal.* This data set spanning 32 years—a rarity in science—concluded that our sun is uncommonly stable.

The sun is a star among countless others, but in many respects it stands alone. It is the perfect lighthouse for the one planet that we know harbors life. Rejoicing like "a strong man to run a race," it journeys across our sky each day, radiating its life-sustaining energy and declaring the glory of God (Psalm 19:1-6).

If the moon were much larger or nearer to the earth, the huge tides that would result would overflow onto the lowlands and erode the mountains. If the continents were leveled, it is estimated that water would cover the entire surface to the depth of over a mile! If the earth was not tilted 23° on its axis, but rather was on a 90° angle in reference to the sun, we would not have four seasons.

Without seasons, life would soon not be able to exist on earth—the poles would lie in eternal twilight, and water vapor from the oceans would be carried by the wind towards both the north and south, freezing when it moved close enough to the poles. In time, huge continents of snow and ice would pile up in the polar regions, leaving most of the earth a dry desert. The oceans would eventually disappear, and rainfall would cease. The accumulated weight of ice at the poles would cause the equator to bulge, and, as a result, the earth's rotation would drastically change.

Just a "little" change (in the perspective of the universe) would render the earth unsuitable to support any life. Is this the result of accidental randomness, or purposeful intent?

The Miracle of Water

What makes the earth so beautiful? Interplay between the light from the sun and the white, blue, green, and brown colors from the earth produce incredible vistas from mountaintops and space. The ocean and atmosphere, the grasses and forests, the mountains and deserts, and the clouds and snow reflect, absorb, and scatter various colors of the rainbow.

The earth is the only known planet with huge bodies of water. Seventy percent of its surface area consists of oceans, lakes, and seas surrounding huge bodies of land. The few planets that have water contain only moisture floating as vapor on their surface or small amounts of ice or liquid water on the planet itself, not large bodies of liquid water as on earth.

Liquid water is necessary for most life processes on the earth and explains why the planet is so fertile. Some of the other planets like Mars may have contained liquid water in the past as evidenced by erosional features, but this water has either evaporated and escaped to space or is trapped in the crust in frozen form.

Water is unique in that it can absorb enormous amounts of heat without a large alteration in its temperature. Its heat absorption level is about ten times as great as steel. During the day, the earth's bodies of water rapidly soak up enormous amounts of heat; thus, the earth stays fairly cool. At night, they release the vast amounts of heat that they absorbed during the day, which, combined with atmospheric effects, keeps most of the surface from freezing solid at night. If it were not for the tremendous amounts of water on the earth, far greater day and night temperature variations would exist. Many parts of the surface would be hot enough to boil water during the day, and the same parts would be cold enough to freeze water at night. Because water is an excellent temperature stabilizer, the large oceans on earth are vital for life to exist on earth.

In contrast to virtually all other materials (the rare exceptions include rubber and antimony), water contracts when cooled only until it reaches 4° Celsius. Then it amazingly expands until it freezes. Thus, because of this anomaly, the ice that forms in seas, oceans, and lakes stays near the surface, where the sun heats it during the day and the warm water below melts it in the summer. This and the Coriolis effect, which produces ocean currents, ensure that most of the ocean stays in a liquid form, allowing the myriad of water creatures to live.

This is one more stunning demonstration that the "LORD by wisdom hath founded the earth; by understanding hath he established the heavens" (Proverbs 3:19). These unique features, all working together to form the properties of this most basic of life-supporting compounds, cannot justly be called "coincidences" or "random accumulations." Water is a created necessity to our planet and to our life.

The Miracle of Air

The mixture of gases usually found in the atmosphere not contaminated by human pollution is perfect for life. If it were much different (e.g., 17 percent instead of 21 percent oxygen, too little carbon dioxide, etc., or the atmospheric pressure were much higher or lower), life would cease to exist on earth.

The air close to the earth's surface is heated by light energy from the sun, and after the air is warmed it becomes less dense and rises upward. The result is that the air near the earth's surface maintains a temperature in which life can exist. If air contracted when heated and became denser, the temperature on the earth's surface would become unbearable, and most life could not survive for very long. The temperature a few hundred feet above the surface, on the other hand, would be extremely cold, and most life could also not exist there for very long. The only habitable region would be a thin slice of air, but even here life could not exist for long because the plants and trees necessary to support the life in the atmosphere could not survive, as they would be in the cold zone. Thus birds would have no resting place, nor would they have food, water, or oxygen. But because air on the earth's surface rises when heated, life can exist on the earth.

The movement of warm air from the surface rising upward creates air currents, which are an important part of the earth's ecological system. These currents (wind) carry away carbon dioxide from areas that overproduce, such as cities, and move oxygen to areas in need of it, such as the large urban population centers.

God has designed the atmosphere to maintain a uniform temperature, whether there is a cooling or a warming tendency. He created the atmosphere with a built-in thermostat that maintains thermal equilibrium.

If our atmosphere were much thinner, many of the millions of meteors that now are burned up would reach the earth's surface, causing death, destruction, and fires everywhere. The contrast becomes even greater when examining the atmospheres of our neighboring planets, Mars and Venus. Unlike earth, Mars has no global magnetic field. High-energy particles impacting a barrier generate showers of secondary particles, causing even more damage. Mars is no place for playful romps. Dust devils meandering over the ultra-dry surface generate highly oxidizing compounds, blanketing the soil with toxic chemicals and charging the dust with static electricity. Fine dust would get into everything, irritating moist membranes and damaging equipment (see *Astronomy*, March 2006). Mars probably smells awful, too, and the atmosphere is so thin, nobody could hear you scream.

Venus is curiously similar to earth, yet profoundly different. Venus has a sultry atmosphere, supersonic winds, a mountain higher than Everest, volcanic flows that look like pancakes, and about a thousand craters—but no plate tectonics and only a weak magnetic field. Our ideas about Venus have made an almost complete about-face since 1960, when many hoped it was a lush, tropical world that might host exotic life.

This hellish world now poses a serious challenge to uniformitarian views. Craters, mountains, and volcanic features all appear to be the same age. Planetary scientists, believing in long ages, have been forced to infer that the first 90 percent of the planet's history is missing!

Evolutionary naturalism is perplexed at what it finds on Mars and Venus—because such reasoning is dependent on trying to figure out how such conditions could come about "naturally" without catastrophic intervention. Such thinking is clouded by the restriction that God does not exist, and that everything came about through random processes over eons of time.

Creationists, on the other hand, find the 90 percent of time "missing" on Venus and the unlivable "thin" atmosphere on Mars nothing more than continued evidence that "the heaven, even the heavens, are the LORD's: but the earth hath he given to the children of men" (Psalm 115:16).

Those who insist on an explanation that excludes God in their thinking will always be perplexed at what they discover. In the meantime, step outside underneath the gentle sun, breathe the sweet air, and thank God for his "wonderful works to the children of men" (Psalm 107:8).

The Unique Environment for Life

If evolution works to transform life to fit the existing environments, why has it not equally conquered all of the various environments here and elsewhere? Earth is the only planet circling our sun on which life as we know it could (and does) exist. A brief glance at the earth and all other known planets finds many startling contrasts. Like no other planet, ours is covered with green vegetation, blue-green seas, streams, rivers, mountains, and deserts which produce a spectacular variety of color and texture—all other known planets are covered with lifeless soil which varies only according to slight movements made by wind or mild air currents.

Earth is far better suited for life than any other planet, yet even here most of the environments are too hot, too cold, too far underground or too far above ground to support much life. In the many thousands of miles of changing environments from the center of the earth to the edge of its atmosphere, there are only a few meters of habitable environment for most life forms, and therefore, almost all creatures are forced to live there. Although in our solar system only the earth was made to be inhabited (Isaiah 45:18), even on the earth only a thin slice is ideally suited for most life forms, including those we are most familiar with, such as mammals, birds, and reptiles.

This thin section, though, is teeming with life. It is estimated that an acre of typical farm soil, six inches deep, has several tons of living bacteria, almost a ton of fungi, two hundred pounds of one-cell protozoan animals, about one hundred pounds of yeast, and the same amount of algae.

The chances of a planet being just the right size, the proper distance away from the right star, etc., are extremely minute, even if many stars have planets circling them, as some speculate. The mathematical odds that all of these and other essential conditions happened by chance are astronomical—something like billions to one!

THE DECLARATION OF THE HEAVENS

Our universe is filled with awesome wonders. There are billions of galaxies, each containing billions of stars, each one named by the Creator (Isaiah 40:26). Even the configurations of the stars in the heavens have a purpose (Job 38:31-33).

> The heavens declare the glory of God; and the firmament sheweth his handywork. Day unto day uttereth speech, and night unto night sheweth knowledge. (Psalm 19:1-2)

God is both omniscient and omnipotent. He has the wisdom to know what is best to do, and the power to accomplish it. Thus, He makes no mistakes and never needs to go back and revise or redirect something He started. What He does is forever!

Many Scriptures (e.g., Psalm 148:1-6) assure us that the sun, moon, and stars, as well as the renewed earth, will continue to function through all the endless ages to come. Nothing can defeat God's primeval purposes in creating them. The Creator of the infinitely complex, highly energized cosmos must necessarily be omniscient and omnipotent. Having created life, as well as human personalities, He must also be a living Person. No effect can be greater than its cause.

Therefore, God is fully capable of revealing to us knowledge about His creation—knowledge which could never be learned through studying present processes. It almost seems that He must do this, in fact, since He surely is not capricious. He would not create men and women who long to know the meaning of their lives, yet neglect or refuse to tell them anything about it.

Giant telescopes of the present day have only begun to reveal the immense numbers and fantastic variety of the stars. With literally billions of galaxies, and billions of stars in every galaxy, the number of the stars seems to be almost without limit. The variety is equally amazing—red giants, white dwarfs, Cepheid variables, neutron stars, pulsars, and on and on! As the Bible says in an amazing preview of modern astronomy: "There is one glory of the sun, and another glory of the moon, and another glory of the stars: for one star differeth from another star in glory" (1 Corinthians 15:41).

The idea of a simple fiat creation of the entire universe in its present form may seem too naïve to evolutionary astronomers and cosmologists. Nevertheless, it fits all the facts of observational astronomy more easily and directly than does any other theory. The objection that special creation is not scientific because it is non-observable is irrelevant, since exactly the same objection applies to any of the evolutionary models. Who has ever observed a star evolve, or a "big bang," or an evolution of matter out of nothing?

There is much to "see" and to "hear" from the heavens. The universe writes the character of God with a broad sweep of His handwriting for all to know. One well-known Christian intellectual and apologist of Jesus' day, the Apostle Paul, wrote: "The invisible things of him from the creation of the world are clearly seen, being understood by the things that are made, even his eternal power and Godhead" (Romans 1:20).

Paul further concludes that those who reject the "speech" and "language" of the universe are "without excuse."

The "Speech" of the Day

The "day unto day" faithfulness of constant stability and dependable processes is a "speech" without words that testifies to God's care and provision.

We have previously touched on the specific wonders of the sun and the moon. These great lights were obviously designed to "rule" the daytime and the nighttime (Genesis 1:16), and their role in "telling" us about God is fairly easy to see if we are not blinded by an insistence on the unprovable position that "there is no God" (Psalm 14:1).

What may often be overlooked by the "day unto day" routine (Psalm 19:1-2) of our existence is that the very dependability of each day's processes are a wonderful testimony to the design, purposes, and faithfulness of the Creator. The whole core of evolutionary naturalism, however, is randomness, an unknowable, undependable chaos and disorder. The universe, on the other hand, is very stable!

- The sun rises in the east and sets in the west—always.
- The earth turns on its axis and cycles through its "day" at the same speed every time—always.
- The dependable clockwork precision of the tides regulates much of our life—always.
- The seasons come and go, the planting and harvesting follow each other dependably, life is conceived and born with regularity, even "natural selection" preserves and conserves the vast species of earth—always.

After the awful judgment of the great Flood of Noah's day, God gave a solemn promise to Noah, and through him to all living creatures. With that promise, God placed in effect the same creative power that brought the universe into existence (Colossians 1:17), but He now focused His grace and mercy on keeping the universe stable until He finalizes His plans for eternity (2 Peter 3:7).

> The LORD said in his heart, I will not again curse the ground any more for man's sake; for the imagination of man's heart is evil from his youth; neither will I again smite any more every thing living, as I have done. While the earth remaineth, seedtime and harvest, and cold and heat, and summer and winter, and day and night shall not cease. (Genesis 8:21-22)

This wordless "language" is easily read by all humanity, and openly "declares" that God is awesomely omnipotent and omniscient, and at the same time lovingly compassionate and faithful. All living creatures depend on it.

The "Knowledge" of the Night

Abundant evidence of God's wisdom and provision can be found within our own galaxy. Unlike many other galaxies, the Milky Way contains just the right balance of stars and planets needed to support life on earth. And our solar system is situated within the Milky Way so that it is far enough from the central region to escape the immense radiation from the stars concentrated there. The lower radiation in our vicinity also gives us a clearer window to observe and study the universe beyond our galaxy.

We live in a time when our knowledge of the heavens is expanding quickly. This knowledge should lead us to praise God for His amazing provision and protection. The cause of the laws of nature is not found in nature, but beyond nature. The heavens declare evidence for creation by their beauty, size, and order.

FOR FURTHER STUDY

The articles listed below are available at www.icr.org. Find the "Search" bar on the opening page of the website, type in the title of the article that you wish to read, and click "Enter." The web search will take you directly to the article.

A Faulty Climate Trigger

A Few Reasons an Evolutionary Origin of Life Is Impossible

Adam and the Animals

Are Plants Alive?

Astrobiology: Follow the...

Biblical Uniformitarianism

Blessings from the Old Files

Blue-t-ful Beetles, Birds, 'n Butterflies

Can Raw Energy Create Order?

Can Research Be Done from a Creation Base?

Carl Sagan's Pale Blue Dot

Christianity and Technological Advance—The Astonishing Connection

Creation and the Environment

Creation by Inflation and Quantum Fluctuation

Crisis in Crater Count Dating

Curiously Wrought

Design Features for the Monarch Butterfly Life Cycle

Design in Nature: The Anthropic Principle

Did the Watchmaker Make the Watch?

Does the Similarity of Human Blood to Sea Water Prove Life Originated in the Ocean?

Earth: A Special Place

Earth's Climate Thermostat

Einstein's Gulf: Can Evolution Cross It?

Evidence for a Young Earth from the Ocean and Atmosphere

Evidence for Global Warming

Evolution Hopes You Don't Know Chemistry: The Problem of Control

Evolution, Thermodynamics, and Entropy

Evolution: The Ocean Says NO!

Exploring the Limitations of the Scientific Method

Food, Fasting, and Physiology

For Every Structure There Is a Reason

Glory and Thanks

God's Library

Habitable Zones

Harsh Unfriendly Mars

Has the Missing Link Been Found?

How Long Will the Sun Last?

I Think, Therefore There Is a Supreme Thinker

If All Animals Were Created as Plant Eaters, Why Do Some Have Sharp Teeth?

Inspired Guesses, Creative Imagination, and Science

Is Man a "Higher Animal"?

Is There Water on the Moon?

Just How Simple Are Bacteria?

Koala Chemistry and Creation

Language, Creation and the Inner Man

Maker and Owner

Mending Mistakes: The Amazing Ability of Repair

More Than a Rising Star

Planet Earth: Plan or Accident?

Reheating the Prebiotic Soup

Running with Birds and Butterflies

Scientific Irrationality

Space Travel? Shields UP!

Spiral Wonder of the Spider Web

Sunlight Before the Sun

Supernova Shell Shock

The Anthropic Principle

The Earth: Unique in All the Universe (Updated)

The Evidence of Nothing

The Finished Works of God

The Flight of Migratory Birds

The Foolishness of Human Wisdom

The Golden Rule

The Gospel of Creation and the Anti-Gospel of Evolution

The Greater Light to Rule the Day

The Logic of Biblical Creation

The Mathematical Impossibility of Evolution

The Migratory Flight of Birds

The Moon: A Faithful Witness in the Sky

The Mystery of the Earth's Magnetic Field

The Outer Darkness

The Plasma Universe

The Pursuit of Happiness

The Splendid Faith of the Evolutionist

The Staff of Life

The Stars of Heaven

The Urge to Submerge

The Wisdom Mine

The Wisdom of This World

The Witness of Conscience

Thinking God's Thoughts After Him

Un-Bee-lievable Vision

Venus vs. Uniformitarianism

What Astronomers Don't Know

What Makes Us Human?

Where Has All the Water Gone?

Where Is Wisdom?

Why Do We Marry? Are All Men Created Equal?

EVIDENCE *from* SCIENCE

*That their hearts might be comforted, being knit together in love,
and unto all riches of the full assurance of understanding,
to the acknowledgement of the mystery of God, and of the
Father, and of Christ; in whom are hid all the
treasures of wisdom and knowledge.*

Colossians 2:2-3

EVIDENCE
from
SCIENCE

E vidence for special creation surrounds us. Everywhere from microscopic elements to the unfathomable recesses of the universe, the Creator speaks to us through the things that He has made.

Where does everything come from and what does it mean? Science is limited in its ability to answer the questions nearest to our hearts. However, science does give us tools to understand our universe and the laws of nature that we can observe today.

This understanding provides compelling evidence for creation.

THE PHYSICAL SCIENCES

The physical universe of space, time, and mass/energy has not always existed, but was supernaturally created by a transcendent personal Creator who alone has existed from eternity. The laws of science demonstrate that mass and energy were created to last. Our place in the universe is perfectly balanced for life.

There are many avenues of science that study the physical laws of mass, energy, and the forces of nature at all levels of scale.

The Universe Demands a Designer

Everyone knows the universe looks designed.

Naturalists want to explain the universe as a necessary outcome of laws and initial conditions, instead of a "roll of the dice." The Big Bang theory, inflation, and the search for structure in the cosmic background radiation are all part of this tradition. The design argument took on renewed urgency in the 1930s when quantum physicists realized that certain constants, like the force of gravity and the charge on the electron, could have taken arbitrary values—yet most values would never produce a universe with atoms, stars, planets, or observers.

One early escape from the design inference was the so-called Anthropic Principle, but most naturalists have dismissed such speculations as metaphysical fluff. However, something was discovered in 1996 that brought cosmologists kicking and screaming back to the Anthropic Principle. The universe is not only expanding, it's accelerating. The acceleration parameter, or cosmological constant, appears so finely tuned (nearly zero, but slightly positive) that almost any larger value would prohibit the formation of stars and galaxies. Theoretical predictions are off by 120 orders of magnitude.

Some hoped that *superstring* theory would come to the rescue, but its champions found that their equations permit 10^{500} different sets of initial conditions—most of them life-prohibiting. The only way our universe could be explained, therefore, was either by a Designer who chose the right values or by luck among untold numbers of alternate universes with random values.

One of the basic axioms in science is the principle of Occam's Razor. In its simplest form, Occam's Razor states that one should make no more assumptions than are needed. That "keep it simple" principle would surely prefer a single Designer to uncountable universes.

Unimaginable Power

Beyond the power that lights the universe with stars is our Creator, who carefully balances the laws of nature. A star is a continuous explosion of awesome power. The power to create a universe with a billion galaxies, each with a billion stars, is beyond imagination. To create mass and energy can only be done by a Creator who is outside of nature.

The creation of the laws of nature themselves demonstrates an even greater power. These laws are balanced so that our sun provides the energy to us day by day. These laws are balanced so that the molecules within us can use that energy.

Exquisite Order

The laws of nature are finely tuned so that our sun can burn and provide us with the energy we need.

Light from stars and the sun begins with hydrogen. Hydrogen is the most plentiful element in the universe. The sun is a large ball of very hot hydrogen. It is more than 100 times larger than the earth. The energy of the sun comes from explosions of hydrogen. These are nuclear explosions, which are much more powerful than chemical explosions.

Gravity draws all the sun's hydrogen together, creating intense pressure. In the core of the sun, the huge forces cause nuclear fusion reactions. Hydrogen atoms fuse together into helium and release huge amounts of energy.

These explosions do not cause the sun to suddenly blow up and then go cold. The balanced laws of physics hold our sun together. Gravity pulls the atoms back as each explosion pushes them away. This balance keeps the billions of stars in billions of galaxies burning.

Absolute Precision

If the laws of nature were just slightly different, the delicate balance would not exist between hydrogen, oxygen, and carbon. Without this balance, thousands of critical molecular interactions would not happen. There are only a few elements that can sustain life through their unique properties. Any change would make life impossible.

The universe is only several thousand years old. Comets are an example of a natural clock within our solar system. With each orbit around the sun, comets lose considerable mass. They cannot be very old because they cannot survive many orbits.

To get around this problem, many astronomers assume there is a vast cloud of comets near the edge of the solar system, which releases new comets every so often. This imaginary cloud is called the Oort Cloud, named after the astronomer who proposed it. The problem is that there is no observational evidence that such a cloud exists at all.

Each year our knowledge of astronomy increases with new evidence concerning the origin of our solar system, our galaxy, and our universe. While it is possible to make assumptions beyond what can be observed and verified, the heavens continue to bear witness to recent creation.

Central Core

Our solar system appears to be near the center of the universe. Galaxies look the same, and are moving away from us in the same way, in all directions. The cosmic microwave background radiation comes to us very uniformly from all directions. These and other data strongly indicate we are located at a very special location by design.

Instead of accepting the obvious, recent models of physical cosmology assume that the earth is not special and that everywhere in the universe the exact same observation of receding objects would be seen. Instead of a universe with an age measured in thousands of years, this assumption leads to billions of years.

In contrast, creation cosmologies explain the data better by starting from biblically-based axioms: the cosmos has a unique center and a boundary for its matter, beyond which there is at least some empty space; and on a cosmic scale of distances, the earth is near the center.

The Universe Is Stable

Energy cannot be created or destroyed; it can only be changed from one form to another. An energy source beyond nature is required. The universe was created sometime in the past and has been decreasing in available energy ever since. The light from distance galaxies confirms that their chemical elements behave in the same way as here on earth.

Energy Can Neither Be Created Nor Destroyed

One of the most basic laws of science is the Law of the Conservation of Energy. Energy cannot be created or destroyed; it can only be changed from one form to another.

Energy is not currently being created. The universe could not have created itself using natural processes because nature did not exist before the universe came into existence. Something beyond nature must have created all the energy and matter that is observed today. Present measures of energy are incredibly enormous, indicating a power source so great that "infinite" is the best word we have to describe it.

The logical conclusion is that a supernatural Creator with infinite power created the universe. There is no other energy source capable of originating what we observe today.

Available Energy Decreases over Time

There is less available energy today than there was yesterday. The Second Law of Thermodynamics states that the entropy of an isolated system, such as the universe, that is not in equilibrium will tend to increase over time, approaching a maximum value at equilibrium. The Third Law of Thermodynamics states that as the temperature approaches absolute zero, the entropy of a system approaches a constant.

Fortunately for us, the temperature of the universe is not zero. It is moving that way each moment, but it is not there yet.

At some prior time, all the energy in the universe was available. Energy must have been created at some finite time in the past; otherwise we would have died long ago.

The logical conclusion is that an infinite Creator made the universe a finite time ago.

Elements Are Dependable across the Universe

The visible energy from the sun is the sunshine that lights the day and the moonlight reflected by the moon at night. The range of visible colors is a very small part of the electromagnetic spectrum. The range of visible light across the spectrum forms the colors we call a rainbow.

Chemicals give off and absorb light at specific points on the electromagnetic spectrum. By comparing the light from various chemicals with the light from our sun, we have learned that our sun is made up mostly of hydrogen. We have also learned which atoms are in galaxies far away. The chemical elements across the universe behave the same as they do for us.

Processes today operate primarily within fixed natural laws and relatively uniform process rates, but since these laws were themselves originally created and are daily maintained by their Creator, there is always the possibility of miraculous intervention in these laws or processes by their Creator.

The Earth Was Uniquely Created

If left to chance, it is unlikely that any place in the universe could support life. God created our planet for life to thrive. As we learn how special our planet is within the entire universe, we learn of our Creator's faithfulness to us.

Our sun has been placed at the perfect location within our galaxy, and our planet has been placed at the perfect location within our solar system. Our planet was created to protect the life that God placed here. Even the atmosphere and oceans of our planet have been carefully designed to provide the right amount of energy and fresh water.

Our Earth Was Created for Life

Our solar system is filled with amazing planets, but none are perfect for life except the earth.

Mercury is the closest planet to the sun. It gets very hot and very cold. It has a very slow spin. The side facing the sun is heated to 800° F while the side away from the sun is cooled to -298° F.

Venus is hotter than Mercury, yet farther away from the sun. Venus has an atmosphere 90 times thicker than earth's. Heat is trapped in the clouds and heats the entire planet to 931° F.

Mars is similar to earth in many ways. A day on Mars is 24.7 hours. It is tilted 25 degrees, just two more degrees than earth. At its warmest, it can get to be a comfortable 67° F. It has two small moons. But Mars is smaller than earth. The gravity on Mars is only a third of earth's. Without enough gravity, Mars is unable to hold a larger atmosphere. What atmosphere it has is made of gases we cannot breathe. Without much of an atmosphere, many meteoroids hit Mars. It also gets very cold at night.

Jupiter is the largest planet in our solar system. It is ten times smaller than the sun and ten times larger than the earth. Jupiter spins faster than any other planet, with a day of 9 hours and 55.5 minutes. Its fast spin causes tremendous storms. The big red spot on Jupiter is actually a huge hurricane.

Saturn is the second largest planet in our solar system and has the largest set of rings. It is almost twice as far away from the sun as Jupiter. Saturn is a gas giant. As one descends into the atmosphere, the pressure, temperature, and gravity greatly increase. The core of the planet is boiling hot and radiates more heat out into space than it receives from the sun.

Uranus is tilted on its side with its axis pointed at the sun. If the earth's axis was pointed at the sun, one hemisphere would always be boiling hot and the other would be freezing cold. Uranus is four times as far from the sun as Jupiter and twice as far from the sun as Saturn.

Neptune is the farthest gas giant from the sun. It is almost four times larger than the earth. Its strong gravity traps harmful gases in its atmosphere.

Each planet in our solar system demonstrates that earth is unique and specially created for life.

Our Sun Is Perfectly Located within Our Galaxy

The spiral-shaped galaxy in which the earth is located is called the Milky Way. The spiraling arms and center of this galaxy contain many stars set close together, giving off its characteristic brightness.

Other galaxies—older, smaller, elliptical, and irregular—are missing the proper amounts of elements necessary to maintain the right balance of stars and planets required to support life.

Some stars explode into supernovas, causing deadly radiation to flow through nearby stars and planets.

The center and arms of galaxies are flooded with high amounts of radiation. Most stars are located in places with too much harmful energy for life. Moreover, at that location we could not observe farther than a few light years into the rest of the universe, because the nearby stars would completely block our view.

Our solar system is located about two-thirds of the way out toward the edge of the Milky Way, where we are least likely to suffer collisions with other stars. Most of the stars in our galaxy are within the larger spiral arms or in the center. Because there are few stars near us, there is a low amount of radiation surrounding our solar system. And we can observe the rest of the universe and our own galaxy much better.

Our Planet Is Perfectly Located within Our Solar System

Our solar system also contains thousands of asteroids and meteoroids. These sometimes collide with planets. Jupiter keeps many large rocks from hitting earth by attracting them with its strong gravity.

The earth's huge moon also protects us from many of the rocks that cross our planet's path. The craters across the moon's surface demonstrate the number of times something has collided with the moon instead of earth. The moon's South Pole Aitken basin is the largest known crater in our solar system. It is 8 miles deep and 1500 miles across. The earth's moon is unusually large.

In addition, our huge moon is a stabilizing anchor for our planet. Our moon prevents our planet from tilting too far from the attraction of the sun or Jupiter.

We are protected by how our solar system was created.

Our Planet Was Created for Life

A smaller planet, like Mars, would be unable to hold our atmosphere, which protects us from meteoroids and keeps the temperature within the range needed for life.

A larger planet, like Neptune, would trap too much atmosphere. The pressure and temperature would greatly increase. A stronger gravity from the increased size would also trap harmful gases in the atmosphere.

Earth has a strong magnetic field. This protects us from harmful radiation from the sun.

Our Water Cycle Protects and Provides

Clouds function as earth's curtains, balancing the temperature. When they form, they block the sun when the temperature on earth becomes too hot and let the sunlight in when it becomes too cold. When the earth is hot, more water evaporates from the oceans and turns into clouds. These clouds reflect more energy and the earth cools. When the earth is cold, the clouds cool and condense into rain and snow. With fewer clouds, less energy is reflected. The energy reaches the earth and warms it. The earth has the most diverse collection of reflective surfaces in our solar system.

Water is the most abundant chemical compound on earth. Water covers three fourths of the earth's surface. Between half to three fourths of your body is water. Water is ideal for carbon-based chemistry.

Water is transported from the ocean to the atmosphere, to the land, and then back to the ocean. The ocean is the primary storehouse of water on the earth. The sun evaporates water from the oceans, which rises into the atmosphere and eventually returns to the ocean.

The atmosphere also stores a small quantity of water. Wind blows water vapor from the hot ocean to the cool land. Cooling water vapor condenses into clouds. Water falls back to the land as rain and snow.

The land also stores water. Fresh water is held for months and years in the form of ice and snow. Water infiltrates the land and is stored underground. Surface water flows into streams and river. Lakes store water. Water flows from the land back into the ocean.

Water expands when it freezes, unlike most other substances. Ice and snow take up more volume than the same amount of liquid water. This makes water denser as a liquid than when it is frozen, so ice floats on the surface. If ice did not float on the surface of the water, the floors of oceans and lakes would be covered with glaciers of ice that never melted. Ice helps regulate the climate by reflecting energy.

As a liquid, water's temperature range is perfect for cycling water from the oceans to the land. Water takes a lot of energy to evaporate into a vapor, and it releases this energy when it condenses back into liquid. This absorption and release of energy balances temperatures in the earth's climate, as well as inside living cells. If less energy were required for evaporation, streams, rivers and lakes would evaporate away quickly.

THE EARTH SCIENCES

Extraordinary geologic processes are key to understanding earth's catastrophic past. Abundant and compelling geologic evidence argues for the global Flood. The fossil record demonstrates stability, complexity, and abrupt appearance—predictions of the creation model. Natural processes tell of a young earth.

The Global Flood Is the Key to the Past

Widespread marine strata and fossils in the earth's highest mountains and upon elevated continental plateaus imply that the ocean once covered the continents. Large geological structures that were quickly formed are worldwide evidence of a global flood. Sedimentary rock beds that were rapidly formed cover the earth. A big, water-based event happened in the recent past to form the geological features we see around us.

The issue of whether or not the worldwide Flood of Noah's day took place as described in the Bible makes an enormous difference in how a geologist or paleontologist looks at the data entombed in the rocks of the earth.

To begin with, the rock strata and fossil remains are the only empirical "clues" that scientists have about the ancient past of earth's history. If indeed the strata were laid down over millions of years, no human was alive to record the events, nor could they be. If, however, the strata were deposited by a global deluge as presented by the information in the Bible, all who are alive today are dependent on the "eyewitness" account of that flood.

Science cannot reproduce the processes. The best that a scientist can do with the unobserved past is to evaluate the "clues" in the rocks and the fossils, and try to understand them in the light of present processes or with the comparison of hydraulic forces on a much smaller scale.

Historical or forensic science is framed by the presuppositional "belief" system that is embraced by the scientist. If the scientist embraces the naturalistic and evolutionary point of view, then he will "interpret" the data in the light of that view. The same is true for a scientist who embraces the biblical point of view. That scientist would look at the same data as the evolutionary scientist, and come to a very different conclusion.

If the biblical account of a global flood is true as the Bible teaches, then most of the rock strata and nearly all of the fossil remains were laid down during one year. If the evolutionary view is true, then the "bias" of present uniformitarian conditions will lead to the conclusion that the time lapse is millions of years.

All science makes "predictions" based on a hypothesis. This is especially true of historical or forensic science, since the scientist was not around to see the actual event take place. The hypothesis that finds the most predictions to be in agreement with the facts is most likely the accurate picture. When predictions about a "model" or "theory" are not corroborated by the data, science would then suggest that the hypothesis is not correct.

Testing the validity of predictions is an important method to verify the accuracy of a theory.

Much Evidence Exists for a Worldwide Flood

History is not open to scientific testing. Geologists, therefore, interpret the geologic record using their limited understanding of modern geologic processes, typically by comparing the record with slow processes known to occur in historic times.

Twentieth-century geologists taught the familiar maximum "The present is the key to the past."

However, geologists in the last 30 years have recognized evidence supporting regional, continental, and global catastrophic events that appear to have formed the major portion of the strata. Natural disasters and their aftermaths have direct application to interpreting the geologic record.

Catastrophist patterns of interpretation have thoroughly permeated conventional thinking about the geologic record; geologists are deliberately reevaluating outdated uniformitarian thinking and are increasingly adopting a global catastrophic model.

But now that catastrophic processes are widely employed to describe the strata record, twenty-first century geologists are wondering whether "marine flood sedimentation is the key to the past."

Strata and the marine fossils they contain provide critical evidence that the ocean once covered the continents, even the highest continental areas. Extremely widespread strata deposits argue for an intercontinental or global flood.

The Sauk Sequence extends throughout North America and appears to extend into Europe. The Tippecanoe Sequence also covers much of North America and may well extend into Europe and Africa. There are also intercontinental redbed sequences, intercontinental tuff beds, and coal-bearing strata cycles.

Granular, water-charged sediment flows result in very rapid stratification. Dilute flows produce thick sequences of plane beds, graded beds, and crossbeds by sustained unidirectional flow. Such flows also produce thick sequences of hummocky beds by sustained bidirectional flow.

Concentrated sediment flows produce thick strata sequences by abrupt deposition from liquefied suspension, or evenly bedded strata by flow transformation to a tractive current.

Since both young and (most) old earth advocates agree that the strata themselves represent short periods of time, an estimate of the length of the non-depositional and erosional periods will give us the approximate time required for the whole. This draws our attention to the upper surface of each layer. Is there evidence that it lay exposed for great ages, or was it quickly covered by the next layer?

These and many other obvious evidences are leading many geologists to construct a global flood model for earth history.

Geological Processes Were Catastrophic

Earth's geologic strata have been characterized by evolutionists as representing millions of years of accumulation of sediments under water. Modern observers are generally willing to recognize evidence of rapid deposition of the strata by catastrophic processes, but insist that long spans of time passed between depositional episodes. During these long ages, erosion may have occurred, but they say the whole package required great ages.

Creationists, on the other hand, consider that the bulk of earth's sedimentary rock accumulated rapidly beneath the waters of the great Flood of Noah's day. One layer followed another in swift succession, sometimes interrupted by brief periods of quiescence, uplift, and erosion. Some time may have passed between depositional events, but these periods were not long, and the bulk of the sedimentary rock record may represent hardly more than one year.

Regional, continental, and global catastrophic processes are so prominent in the geologic record that many geologists are reorganizing their thinking to better discern and understand these extraordinary events.

Looking like sand on a seashore, many layers exhibit "ripple marks." Yet ripple marks in loose sand last only until the next tide. Even in hard rock they erode within a few years. Their nearly ubiquitous presence on sandstone surfaces argues for quick burial, perhaps by the next wave, protecting them until they hardened.

A similar line of reasoning notes that animal burrows and plant roots, etc., can be found on every modern soil surface, on land or in water. Why are they rare to non-existent in the geologic record? Sometimes a fossil tree or animal body will intersect more than one layer. Called "polystrate" fossils, they demand a short time between layer depositions.

An erosional surface in the rocks is called an unconformity, and some amount of time is necessary between two unconformable layers. But unconformities are not found worldwide. When traced laterally they often grade into conformity, implying continual (rapid) deposition of the sequence. On a larger scale, entire geologic periods like the Cambrian or Ordovician are present, implying a short duration. Sometimes they grade conformably into the next period.

From the Cambrian period upward, the geologic strata are a record of continuous, catastrophic, rapid deposition under flood waters. This is what we would expect based on the biblical account of the great Flood.

Geological Evidence Indicates Rapid Formation

There is extensive evidence for the layers of strata in the geologic record being laid down very quickly, similar to the processes observed when Mount St. Helens erupted. Rapid global formation of sedimentary rock beds is evidence that the earth is thousands, not millions, of years old.

The major formations of the earth's crust are sedimentary rock beds. These were formed by rapid erosion, transportation, and deposition by water. There is no global evidence of great lengths of time between these layers or indications that these layers took long periods of time to form.

For example, sandstone is a major feature of the lower part of the Grand Canyon. The same rock layer is found in Utah, Wyoming, Montana, Colorado, South Dakota, the Midwest, the Ozarks, and in northern New York state. Equivalent formations are found across wide portions of Canada, eastern Greenland, and Scotland.

Skeptics of creation science often claim that no evidence for the Flood exists. Even though most geologists have abandoned old-style uniformity in favor of a grudging acceptance of major catastrophism, they still deny the global, year-long, cataclysm of Noah's day described in Scripture.

Obviously, we can't observe that past event, but if such a world-restructuring flood occurred, what would we expect to result from it?

When considering non-repeatable events of the past, we are limited to scientific "predictions": not predictions of the future, but predictions of the evidence. Reasoning from the biblical record, we would "predict" that when we examine the geologic results of the Flood, we will see that the geologic strata were deposited by catastrophic processes, operating on a regional scale. These large-scale results would dominate the rock record. Uniformitarian scientists would predict that the record would be dominated by the rather slow and gradual geologic processes observed today, operating on a local scale. Once both sides have made their predictions, the evidence can be evaluated as to which one is the better fit. That one is more likely correct.

Consider the Columbia River Basalt Group of lava flows in Washington, Oregon, and Idaho. This series of lava flows was stacked one on top of another in rapid succession and covers an area of some 65,000 square miles, with a volume of about 40,000 cubic miles. This dwarfs the largest historic lava flow, which occurred in Iceland in 1783 and covered an area of about 200 square miles, with a volume of less than 3 cubic miles. One can scarcely envision such eruptions, which produced a veritable "lake of lava" thousands of times larger than anything witnessed by modern men. The molten material flowed from several locations along linear cracks in the earth's surface, but even this deposit is dwarfed by other much larger basalt deposits that have been recognized.

Occurring in layers stratigraphically below the Columbia River Basalts are thick layers of water-deposited, fossil-bearing, sedimentary rock, obviously deposited by the Flood itself. Thus, Flood advocates interpret these mega-eruptions of basalt as probably occurring during the very last stages of the Flood or in the years of readjustment that followed, as earth's systems regained the relative equilibrium in which we now find them. Surely this was a fearful time.

Obviously such large-scale volcanism does not match uniformitarian predictions regarding the past. Yet it does match the creation/Flood/young earth prediction of catastrophic processes operating on a regional scale during and immediately following the Flood. While neither side can directly observe the past, the biblical model is the one that best predicts the evidence, and, is thus, from a scientific perspective, more likely correct.

Worldwide Catastrophic Evidence Is Everywhere

Tremendous amounts of water moving very quickly have left scars throughout the earth's major formations. Catastrophic displacements of enormous plates of the earth's crust provided the driving force for the global Flood and produced the deep spaces for the oceans to drain into afterward.

The majority of our planet's sedimentary rock appears to have accumulated rapidly by means of a worldwide deluge. Single layers were quickly formed that covered large parts of the globe. Fault surfaces that contain zones characterized by microbreccias and pseudotachylite are evidences for rapid displacements.

Beveled surfaces below, within, and above thick strata sequences provide evidence of rapid flood and post-flood erosion. Sheetform beveled surfaces below and within thick strata sequences provide evidence of widespread sediment sublimation during a global flood (e.g., the paraconformity between Coconino Sandstone and Hermit Shale on Bright Angel Trail in the Grand Canyon).

As further evidence for the worldwide nature of the Flood, ancient human cultures across the globe appear to possess legends recounting a great global flood. It is logical that such a cataclysmic event would be carried forward in human memory, with its echoes still sounding today.

Fossils Show Stasis and Not Transitional Forms

The fossil record demonstrates abrupt appearance, complexity at all stratigraphic levels, and maintenance of defining characteristics (or stasis). These primary features of the fossil record are predictions of the creation model.

According to evolution models for the fossil record, there are three main predictions:

- Wholesale change of organisms through time
- Primitive organisms gave rise to complex organisms
- Gradual derivation of new organisms produced transitional forms

Obviously, these two positions and their predictions are opposites, and cannot be merged into some sort of hybrid theory. A careful scientist would use these predictions to evaluate the available evidence to determine which model is the most correct.

Rules of Evidence

Over the past centuries, the search for truth in science has been formalized into the process known as the scientific method. Theories are developed and tested according to a generally accepted standard. In a similar fashion, the legal profession operates by what is known as the Rules of Evidence. In legal controversies, the Rules of Evidence serve as a vital vehicle for seriously searching out and reliably reaching (it is hoped) the truth. Real truth stands up to being tested. And even the absence of evidence can operate as a silent witness, testifying to a circumstance where there is nothing, when there should be something.

Circumstantial Evidence of "Nothing"

In a Medicare fraud case involving years of federal court proceedings, one of the appeals was finally decided in 2007. Part of the convicting evidence was nothing—literally nothing—when there should have been something.

From a circumstantial evidence standpoint, the government's proof of "nothing" (in this case, missing verification of the fraudulent doctor's treatment of patients) clearly demonstrated that the doctor had not provided the "evidence" that he had indeed cared for the people for whom he had billed the Medicare system.

This illustrates the power of an argument from silence—the forensic force of such a silent witness can buttress a sentence of felony jail time. So, technically speaking, how can "nothing" become admissible circumstantial evidence at trial? Federal Evidence Rule 803(10) provides one such forensic possibility. Essentially, the absence of a record, or the nonoccurrence or nonexistence of a matter that would normally have been recorded, can serve as evidence in its own right, provided that a sufficiently diligent search failed to disclose the record.

Evidence Rule 803(7) is similar, but it applies to records that have a relevant "absence" of an entry, as well as where and when a documentary "nothing" is forensically important.

What would happen if we applied the same principles of the Evidence Rules to analyzing the scientific controversies about origins?

Origins and the Evidence of Nothing

So how does the evidence of nothing demonstrated by this particular Medicare fraud scheme relate to the question of origins? The comparison can be illustrated by applying the Evidence Rules that govern "nothing, when there should be something" to the problem of "missing links." This evidentiary insight may be unusual, but it is certainly not new.

When examining the quest for missing links, the evidence is not there—literally nothing, when there should have been something. To use the logic of Rule 803(10), a diligent search for these so-called transitional form fossils over a period of 150 years has failed to disclose them. These years of diligent search indicate a glaring absence of molecules-to-man evolutionary phylogeny in the fossil record. In other words, the empirical data of earth's fossils, if analyzed forensically, show that evolutionary development is just empty imaginings, refuted by the evidence of nothing.

Evolutionists often speak of missing links. They say that the bridge between man and the apes is the "missing link," the hypothetical ape-like ancestor of both. But there are supposed missing links all over the evolutionary tree. For instance, dogs and bears are thought to be evolutionary cousins, related to each other through a missing link. The same could be said for every other stop on the tree. All of the animal types are thought to have arisen by the transformation of some other animal type, and at each branching node is a missing link, and between the node and the modern form are many more. If you still don't know what a missing link is, don't worry. No one knows what a missing link is, because they are missing! We've never seen one.

This argument from silence is an *absence* in the evidentiary record—a "nothing, where there should be something" if evolutionary theory were true. But evolutionary theory is not true, so the real world's fossil record has been providing irrefutable evidence, by the *absence* of missing links, for a long, long time.

Some may say that the above analysis is "much ado about nothing." However, there is so much "science falsely so called" involved that it is imperative that we use the greatest care and the highest standards in our quest to uncover the true history of our world. And sometimes, "nothing" is itself evidence for the truth.

Fossils Show the Immediate Appearance of Complex Life

The fossil record reflects the original diversity of life, not an evolving tree of increasing complexity. When a fossil appears in the sedimentary rock layers, it appears in a fully developed form, with no, repeat *no*, evidence for a transitional ancestor at all.

Trilobites, for instance, appear suddenly in the fossil record without any transitions. There are no intermediate fossils between simple single-cell organisms, such as bacteria, and complex invertebrates, such as trilobites. Extinct trilobites had as much organized complexity as any of today's invertebrates. In addition to trilobites, billions of other fossils have been found that suddenly appear, fully formed, such as clams, snails, sponges, and jellyfish. Over 300 different body plans are found without any fossil transitions between them and single-cell organisms.

Fish have no ancestors or transitional forms to show how invertebrates, with their skeletons on the outside, became vertebrates with internal skeletons.

Fossils of a wide variety of flying and crawling insects appear without any transitions. Dragonflies, for example, appear suddenly in the fossil record. The highly complex systems that enable the dragonfly's aerodynamic abilities have no ancestors in the fossil record.

Evolutionists sometimes brag that they have abundant evidence of transitions, but when pressed, the examples are almost always minor variations within a category that fall within the normal variation expected in living kinds, and are certainly not proof of evolution.

In general, evolutionists are quick to admit the almost complete lack of transitional fossils. In fact, many of the current leaders in evolutionary thought have made their careers attempting to explain this lack by proposing that evolution of isolated groups occurred so rapidly in the past that no individuals of the in-between forms were fossilized. Why should we expect to find fossils of organisms that existed only for a short time? Furthermore, they point out that fossilization rarely occurs today—it usually takes massive flooding and rapid burial.

However, these proponents of "punctuated equilibrium" have no explanation for how such rapid evolution could have taken place. In the end, they are left with the same situation as those who believe in slow, gradual evolution—no evidence.

In the entire fossil record, there is not a single unequivocal transition form proving a causal relationship between any two species. From the billions of fossils we have discovered, there should be thousands of clear examples if they existed.

This lack of transitions between species in the fossil record is what would be expected if life was created.

Fossils Show Rapid and Catastrophic Burial

Fossils universally provide evidence of rapid burial, even agonizing death. Beveled surfaces below, within, and above thick strata sequences provide evidence of rapid flood and post-flood erosion. Rapid burial is necessary to entomb organisms as the first step in fossilization. The abundant marine invertebrate fossils throughout the entire fossil strata demonstrate extraordinary burial conditions.

Very few fossils are forming today, and then only in the case of rapid burial by water. For instance, what happens to a fish when it dies? It either floats to the surface or sinks to the bottom, where it decays and is eaten by scavengers. Yet many fish fossils are so exquisitely preserved that even the scales and organs are preserved. Obviously there was no time for decay and bacterial action. We can certainly say that something extraordinary happened to form the fossils. Furthermore, most fossils occur in huge fossil graveyards where things from different habitats are mixed together in a watery grave. The predominant type of fossil is that of marine invertebrates, but these are found on the continents within catastrophically-deposited rock units.

Of the several different kinds of fossils, each one requires rapid burial and circumstances which are seldom, if ever, at work today.

Polystrate fossil logs (tree trunks in vertical positions running through several sedimentary layers) are common in the fossil layers and are clear evidence of rapid burial. The term "polystrate" was coined to describe a fossil which is encased within more than one (poly) layer of rock (strata), thus "polystrate" or "many layers." A wonderful story can be told by these fossils which invalidates the commonly held uniformitarian idea of the slow and gradual accumulation of sediments.

These "many layered" fossils are the exception to the rule, but are known to all geologists. Frequently, trees are found protruding out of coal seams into the strata above, and perhaps extending into a second coal seam several feet above the first. Such fossils (or their remaining impressions) are found in many coal mines. There are also thin, reed-like stems, transgressing numerous layers. Furthermore, there are hundreds of individual fossils whose body widths exceed the width of the banded layers in which they are encased.

Obviously, the layers cannot be the result of slow accumulations. A dead fish, for example, will not remain in an articulated condition for several years while sediment accumulates around it. No, it must be quickly buried in order to be preserved at all. Some of the big polystrate trees transgress strata otherwise thought to have required tens of thousands of years. Obviously, the entire section required less time than it takes a tree to rot and fall over.

It has now been well demonstrated that rapidly-moving, sediment-laden fluids can result in an abundance of laminations and/or layers. They can be formed in lab experiments, by hurricanes, and were even formed by catastrophic mud flows associated with the eruption of Mount St. Helens.

Common vertebrate fossils also show rigor mortis and postures indicative of asphyxiation—sudden smothering of the animal (e.g., Archaeopteryx and dinosaur fossils in the quarry at Dinosaur National Monument). This is hardly consistent with an evolutionary explanation of the fossil record.

Fossils Are Found at All Levels

The layers of sedimentary rock that cover the earth's surface contain marine creatures at all levels that appear suddenly and fully formed. The earth is covered with layers of sedimentary rock, which were formed from the sediment deposited by enormous water and mud flows. Those continent-covering, water-deposited layers contain countless fossils.

As it turns out, 95 percent of all fossils are shallow marine invertebrates, mostly shellfish. For instance, clams are found in the bottom layer, the top layer, and every layer in between. There are many different varieties of clams, but clams are in every layer and resemble the clams that are still alive today. There is no evolution, just clams! The same could be said for corals, jellyfish, and many others. The fossil record documents primarily marine organisms buried in marine sediments, which (as discussed elsewhere) were catastrophically deposited.

Of the 5 percent remaining fossils, 95 percent of these are algae and plant fossils (4.75 percent of the total). In that left over 5 percent of the 5 percent, insects and all other invertebrates make up 95 percent (0.2375 percent of the total).

All of the vertebrate fossils considered together (fish, amphibians, reptiles, birds, and mammals), comprise only 0.0125 percent of the entire fossil record, and only 1 percent of these, or .000125 percent of the total, consist of more than a single bone! Almost all of them come from the Ice Age. Surely, the vertebrate fossil record is far from complete.

When we look at the invertebrates, we see separate and distinct categories (i.e., clams, corals, trilobites, etc.) existing in the earliest strata with no hint of ancestors or of intermediates. We find clams by the trillions, with a lot of variety among them, but no evolution. Furthermore, we have no idea how vertebrate fish could have arisen from any invertebrate. Where there are good data, we see no evolution. Where the data are scanty, evolutionists create a story. The fossil record is voluminous and apparently substantially complete. Yet no evolution is seen.

The entire record of visible fossils consists mainly of marine invertebrates (animals without a backbone), including clams, jellyfish, and coral. What is surprising is that these ocean creatures are found primarily on the continents and rarely in the deep ocean basins. More clam shells are found on mountain peaks than under the ocean floor.

From the bottom layers to the top layers, most fossils are marine creatures. The upper levels do have an increasing number of vertebrates, such as fish and amphibians, reptiles, and mammals, but the fossils at the bottom levels are equally as complex as any animal today. All fossil types appear suddenly, fully formed and fully functional, without less complex ancestors under them.

The fossil record is strong evidence for the sudden appearance of life by creation, followed by rapid burial during a global flood.

Many Earth "Clocks" Indicate a Recent Creation

How is it possible to visualize a billion years of time? The United States was founded a little over 200 years ago. Columbus discovered Americas some 500+ years ago. These events seem long ago, but the numbers are comparatively small. Continuing back in history, dates are less precise, but the pyramids in Egypt were built about 4,000 years ago. The Asian empires were founded around the same time.

All of these events are rightly relegated to "ancient history." Archaeological artifacts and structures give only nebulous insights into the times of their origin. But in each of these cases we have at least some written history to aid us, scanty though it may be. For times greater than these, the only reliable source we have is the biblical record. According to it, no civilization or record other than itself could exist before the great Flood of Noah's day, and indeed, all ancient legends (i.e., post-flood memories of pre-flood events) are fraught with illogic and mythology.

The Bible even places the creation of all things less than 2,000 years before the Flood. Our minds struggle with the antiquity implied in these long thousands of years.

But can we comprehend one billion years? One billion seconds is approximately 32 years. One billion minutes takes us to the time of Christ. One billion hours is about 115,000 years—beyond any true comprehension. One billion days is nearly three million years. Think about it. What could one billion days possibly mean to an old man who has lived just 30,000 days?

One billion years cannot be grasped; neither can 4.67 billion years for the supposed age of the earth or 14 billion years or so since the so-called Big Bang. The invariable accompaniment of the outward rolling of the hands, suggest that tales of "billions and billions" of years are nothing more than arm-waving, perhaps capable of impressing or intimating, but not of communicating understandable information.

A billion years might just as well be eternity, an equally unfathomable time word. Eternity future we can't comprehend either, but we believe it, because the Creator of time promised it to us.

Measuring the rate at which worldwide processes function provides a "clock" by which the age of the earth may be calculated. Many of these processes yield thousands of years, rather than billions.

The Earth's Magnetic Field Is Decaying Too Fast

The total energy stored in the earth's magnetic field ("dipole" and "non-dipole") is decreasing with a half-life of 1,465 (± 165) years. Evolutionary theories explaining this rapid decrease, as well as how the earth could have maintained its magnetic field for billions of years, are very complex and inadequate.

A much better theory exists within creation science. It is straightforward, based on sound physics, and explains many features of the field. This theory matches paleomagnetic, historic, and present data, most startlingly with evidence for rapid changes. The main result is that the field's total energy (not surface intensity) has always decayed at least as fast as now. At that rate the field could not be more than 20,000 years old.

Many Strata Are Too Tightly Bent

In many mountainous areas, strata thousands of feet thick are bent and folded into hairpin shapes. The conventional geologic time scale says these formations were deeply buried and solidified for *hundreds of millions of years* before they were bent. Yet the folding occurred without cracking, with radii so small that the entire formation had to be still wet and unsolidified when the bending occurred. This implies that the folding occurred less than thousands of years after deposition.

Biological Material Decays Too Fast

Natural radioactivity, mutations, and decay degrade DNA and other biological material rapidly. Measurements of the mutation rate of mitochondrial DNA recently forced researchers to revise the age of "mitochondrial Eve" from a theorized 200,000 years down to possibly as low as 6,000 years. DNA experts insist that DNA cannot exist in natural environments longer than 10,000 years, yet intact strands of DNA appear to have been recovered from fossils allegedly much older: "Neanderthal" bones, insects in amber, and even from dinosaur fossils. Bacteria allegedly 250 million years old apparently have been revived with no DNA damage. Soft tissue and blood cells from a dinosaur have astonished experts.

Too Much Carbon 14 in Deep Geologic Strata

With their short 5,700-year half-life, no carbon 14 atoms should exist in any carbon older than 250,000 years. Yet it has proven impossible to find any natural source of carbon below Pleistocene (Ice Age) strata that does not contain significant amounts of carbon 14, even though such strata are supposed to be *millions or billions of years* old. Conventional carbon 14 laboratories have been aware of this anomaly since the early 1980s, have striven to eliminate it, and are unable to account for it. The world's best laboratory, which has learned during two decades of low C-14 measurements how not to contaminate specimens externally, under contract to creation scientists, confirmed such observations for coal samples and even for a dozen diamonds, which cannot be contaminated *in situ* with recent carbon. These constitute very strong evidence that the earth is only thousands, not billions, of years old.

Diamonds Have Too Much Carbon 14

Natural diamonds are believed to have been formed deep underground in the upper mantle of the earth's crust. Under extreme temperature and pressure, pure carbon is formed into the diamond's crystalline form. Over time, the diamond is moved upwards by rising magma. Natural diamonds are commonly believed to have been formed millions of years ago.

Here is a significant problem for the supposed long ages: carbon 14 has been measured within natural diamonds.

If the rate that carbon 14 decays has been consistent, any carbon 14 older than 100,000 years is undetectable by current measuring techniques.

But carbon 14 is present within natural diamonds. That means either the decay rate of carbon 14 is not uniform, the diamonds are younger than believed, or both. Carbon 14 in diamonds is evidence that the earth is thousands of years old, not millions.

Minerals Have Too Much Helium

Granite is one of the more common rock formations on the earth. The shiny black specks in granite are mica. Within mica are natural zircon crystals, only a few microns in size. As the zircon crystals are forming, they capture uranium and thorium atoms inside the crystal. Uranium and thorium generate helium atoms as they decay to lead. Helium quickly diffuses out of zircon.

A study published in the *Journal of Geophysical Research* showed that such helium produced in zircon crystals in deep, hot pre-Cambrian granitic rock has not had time to escape. Though the rocks supposedly contain *1.5 billion years'* worth of nuclear decay products, newly-measured rates show that helium loss from zircon has been leaking for only a few thousand years.

If the granite is millions of years old, as commonly believed, all the helium should be gone. However, measurements indicate that much of the helium still remains. Either the diffusion rate of the helium is not uniform, the zircon crystals are younger than believed, or both. This is not only evidence for the youth of the earth, but also for episodes of greatly accelerated decay rates of long half-life nuclei within thousands of years ago, compressing radioisotope timescales enormously.

Helium in granite is evidence that the earth is thousands of years old, not millions.

Not Enough Mud on the Sea Floor

Each year, water and wind erode about 20 billion tons of dirt and rock from the continents and deposit it in the ocean. This material accumulates as loose sediment on the hard basaltic (lava-formed) rock of the ocean floor. The average depth of all the sediment in the whole ocean is less than 400 meters. The main way known to remove the sediment from the ocean floor is by plate tectonic subduction. That is, the sea floor slides slowly (a few cm/year) beneath the continents, taking some sediment with it. According to secular scientific literature, that process presently removes only 1 billion tons per year. As far as anyone knows, the other 19 billion tons per year simply accumulate. At that rate, erosion would deposit the present mass of sediment in less than 12 million years.

Yet according to evolutionary theory, erosion and plate subduction have been going on as long as the oceans have existed, an alleged *three billion years*. If that were so, the rates above imply that the oceans would be massively choked with sediment dozens of kilometers deep. An alternative explanation from creation science is that erosion from the waters of the Genesis Flood running off the continents deposited the present amount of sediment within a short time about 5,000 years ago.

The Sea Does Not Have Enough Minerals

Every year, more salt enters the ocean from rivers. At present rates, seawater is not as salty as it should be if the oceans were ancient. There is not enough salt in the sea or mud on the sea floor for the seas to be billions of years old.

Every year, salt accumulates in the ocean from rivers. Given the present rate it is increasing per year, the current 3.5 percent salinity of seawater is much too low if this process has been going on for a very long time.

All Measurement "Clocks" Depend on Unprovable Assumptions

It should be recognized that it is impossible to determine with certainty any date prior to the beginning of historical records—except, of course, by divine revelation. Science, in the proper sense, is based on observation, and we have no past records of observation except historical records. Natural processes can be used to *estimate* prehistoric dates, but not to *determine* such dates. The accuracy of the estimates will depend on the validity of the assumptions applied to the use of the processes in making such calculations.

Any geochronometric calculation is based on at least the following assumptions:

- Constant process rate (or known functional variation of process rate)
- Closed process system (or known external effects on the open system)
- Initial process components known

Not one of these three vital assumptions is provable, or testable, or reasonable, or even possible! Therefore, no geochronometric calculation can possibly be certain, and most of them are bound to be vastly in error.

Since the magnitude of the error in the assumptions obviously will vary quite widely from process to process, one would expect to get a wide range of "apparent ages" from different processes.

The article "The Young Earth" (available on ICR's website) explains the calculations necessary to arrive at "origin" dates and lists 76 different processes for calculating the age of various integral parts of the earth. All of them yield an age of much less than the present standard evolutionary estimate of approximately five billion years.

THE LIFE SCIENCES

There were no human witnesses to the origin of life, and no physical geological evidence of its origin exists.

That pretty well summarizes the extent of the progress evolutionists have made toward establishing a mechanistic, atheistic scenario for the origin of life after more than half a century of physical, chemical, and geological research.

It is possible, however, to derive facts that establish beyond doubt that an evolutionary origin of life on this planet would have been impossible. The origin of life could only have resulted from the action of an intelligent agent external to and independent of the natural universe.

The phenomenon of life did not develop by natural processes from inanimate systems. The first human beings were specially created in fully human form from the start. Biological life was specially and supernaturally created by the Creator.

Life Simply Could Not Just "Happen"

Here a few of the insuperable barriers to an evolutionary origin of life.

The Absence of the Required Atmosphere

Our present atmosphere consists of 78 percent nitrogen (N_2), 21 percent molecular oxygen (O_2), and 1 percent of other gases, such as carbon dioxide (CO_2), argon (Ar), and water vapor (H_2O). An atmosphere containing free oxygen would be fatal to all origin of life schemes. While oxygen is necessary for life, free oxygen would oxidize and thus destroy all organic molecules required for the *origin* of life. Thus, in spite of much evidence that the earth has always had a significant quantity of free oxygen in the atmosphere, evolutionists persist in declaring that there was no oxygen in the earth's early atmosphere. However, *this would also be fatal to an evolutionary origin of life.* If there were no oxygen, there would be no protective layer of ozone surrounding the earth. The deadly destructive ultraviolet light from the sun would pour down on the surface of the earth unimpeded, destroying those organic molecules required for life, reducing them to simple gases, such as nitrogen, carbon dioxide, and water.

Evolutionists face an irresolvable dilemma: in the presence of oxygen, life could not evolve; without oxygen, thus no ozone, life could not evolve or exist.

All Forms of Raw Energy Are Destructive

The energy available on a hypothetical primitive earth would consist primarily of radiation from the sun, with some energy from electrical discharges (lightning), and minor sources of energy from radioactive decay and heat.

The problem for evolution is that the rates of destruction of biological molecules by all sources of raw energy vastly exceed their rates of formation by such energy. The rapid decomposition of those supposed "building blocks" of life would eliminate any possibility of them accumulating enough organic compounds—no matter how much time might be available.

Even if the "primitive" ocean was chock full of organic compounds, the proven principles of chemical thermodynamics and kinetics would eliminate even the possibility of lifeless coacervates forming.

An Evolutionary Origin of Life Would Result in Nothing But Clutter

Let us suppose that there actually was some way for organic, biologically important molecules to have formed in a significant quantity on a primitive earth. An indescribable mess would have been the result.

In addition to the 20 different amino acids found in proteins today, hundreds of other kinds of amino acids would have been produced. In addition to the five-carbon sugars found in DNA and RNA today, a variety of other five-carbon sugars, four-carbon, six-carbon, and seven-carbon sugars would have been produced. In addition to the five purines and pyrimidines required in DNA and RNA, a large number of other purines and pyrimidines would exist.

The amino acids in proteins are exclusively left-handed, but all amino acids on the primitive earth would be 50 percent left-handed and 50 percent right-handed. The sugars in DNA and RNA today are exclusively right-handed, but, if they did exist, sugars on a primitive earth would have been 50 percent right-handed and 50 percent left-handed. If just one right-handed amino acid is in a protein, or just one left-handed sugar is found in a DNA or RNA, all biological activity is destroyed.

There would be no mechanism available on a primitive earth to select the correct form. This fact alone destroys evolution. All these many varieties would compete with one another, and a great variety of other organic molecules, including aldehydes, ketones, acids, amines, lipids, carbohydrates, etc., would exist. Evolutionists have been wrestling with this dilemma since it was first recognized, and there is no solution in sight.

Micromolecules Do Not Spontaneously Combine to Form Macromolecules

The formation of a molecule requires the input of a highly selected type of energy and the steady input of the building blocks required to form it. To produce a protein, the building blocks are amino acids. For DNA and RNA these building blocks are nucleotides, which are composed of purines, pyrimidines, sugars, and phosphoric acid. If amino acids are dissolved in water they do not spontaneously join together to make a protein. That would require an input of energy. If proteins are dissolved in water, the chemical bonds between the amino acids slowly break apart, releasing energy.

To form a protein in a laboratory, the chemist must dissolve the required amino acids in a solvent, and then add a chemical that contains high energy bonds. The energy from this chemical is transferred to the amino acids. This provides the necessary energy to form the chemical bonds between the amino acids and releases H and OH to form water. This only happens in a chemistry laboratory or in the cells of living organisms. It could never have taken place in a primitive ocean or anywhere on a primitive earth.

Evolutionists persistently claim that the initial stage in the origin of life was the origin of a self-replicating DNA or RNA molecule. There is no such thing as a self-replicating molecule, and no such molecule could ever exist.

DNA Could Not Survive Without Repair Mechanisms

DNA, as is true of messenger-RNA, transfer-RNA, and ribosomal-RNA, is destroyed by a variety of agents, including ultraviolet light, reactive oxygen species, alkylting agents, and water. Note that even water is one of the agents that damages DNA! Thus water and many chemical agents dissolved in it, along with ultraviolet light, would destroy DNA much faster than it could be produced by the wildest imaginary process.

There are 130 known human DNA repair genes and more are expected to be found. If it were not for DNA repair genes, DNA could not survive even in the protective environment of a cell. How then could DNA survive when subjected to brutal attack by all the chemical and other DNA-damaging agents that would exist on the hypothetical primitive earth?

DNA is necessary for the survival of DNA! Therefore it would have been impossible for DNA repair genes to evolve before ordinary DNA evolved, and it would have been impossible for ordinary DNA to evolve before DNA repair genes had evolved. This is another impossible barrier for evolution.

The Natural Direction of Life Is Degeneration, Not Evolution

Damage to the genome shortens the lifespan of both individuals and entire populations. As time passes, genetic information erodes.

Mutations in the genomes of organisms are typically nearly neutral, with little effect on the fitness of the organism. However, the accumulation of deleterious (harmful) mutations does occur and the accumulation of these mutations leads to genetic degeneration. Mutations lead to the loss of genetic information and consequently the loss of genetic potential.

This results in what is termed "genetic load" for a population of organisms. Genetic load is the amount of mutation in a kind of organism that affects its fitness for a particular environment. As genetic load increases, the fitness decreases and the organism progresses towards extinction as it is unable to compete with other organisms for resources such as food and living space.

An increase in genetic potential through mutation has not been observed, while the increase in genetic load via mutation is observable in all organisms, and especially in man.

Life Was Created Fully Functional and Immutable

Given all the impossibilities for any evolutionary or purely naturalistic scenario to explain the origin of life, the most logical inference is that life was created by an omnipotent and omniscient "First Cause" that transcends our universe.

DNA Was Created as a Reservoir for the Information of Life

The complex language system that stores life's blueprints demands an author. For life to exist, an information system is needed to produce and regulate life functions. This information system must also be able to accurately copy itself for the next generation. DNA (deoxyribonucleic acid) is the information system for life.

Information is a product of intelligence, indicating that DNA came from an intelligent source (the Creator).

DNA was created with the information to produce proteins for cellular reactions and the ability to copy itself. DNA uses an intermediate, RNA (ribonucleic acid), to transfer this information to the cell machinery to form proteins.

There are several layers of information in DNA. DNA has the genetic code, or code of life, to spell out proteins, but the code is also arranged to minimize errors in protein sequence and structure, regulate the amount of proteins produced in the cell, and assist proteins in folding into the correct shape.

Changes in the information in DNA are called *mutations,* which adversely affect the cell and organism.

Proteins Were Created to Catalyze the Reactions of Life

Life not only requires information, but the ability to control or catalyze chemical reactions. Proteins known as enzymes do this for all living things. Without enzymes, life would not be possible, even in the presence of DNA.

Proteins are formed from long chains of amino acids. There are approximately 20 different amino acids found in living systems. There are several important characteristics that indicate that protein formation from amino acids requires information. Amino acids in living systems are all left-handed, a property called *chirality.* Amino acids must also be activated in order to be linked together to form proteins. Activation requires more enzymes to form the amino acid chains necessary to make proteins. Proteins must also be folded into the correct shape or they will not be functional, requiring additional information for the correct shape for a specific protein.

DNA and proteins work together to make a cell function normally. Mutations can lead to changes in the amino acid sequence in proteins. Just one change in the amino acid sequence in a protein can cause diseases such as cystic fibrosis and sickle cell anemia. These mutations do not lead to more advanced organisms but to organisms that are less fit for survival.

Cells Protect Life Systems

Cells represent the very existence of physical life and come from similar pre-existing life. For DNA and proteins to function properly, a barrier must surround these molecules to prevent unwanted reactions with the chemicals in the environment. As expected, DNA has the information to maintain this barrier, the cell membrane, and proteins provide the catalyst for carrying out the reactions necessary for building and maintaining this barrier. Information in DNA also constructs the cell membrane so that it selects substances useful to the cell and protects against those that will cause harm. These three factors—DNA information, protein catalysts (enzymes), and a protective environment—are all required simultaneously for life to exist as cells.

Cells also represent the very existence of physical life, an observation that led to the Cell Theory:

- All living things are made of cells.
- All cells come from similar pre-existing cells.
- Cells perform the functions of all living things.

From this simple observation, it is clear that life comes from similar pre-existing life (a theory termed biogenesis) and not from non-living material or unrelated life forms. Scripture tells us that ultimately all life originated from Christ (John 1).

Natural Selection and Adaptation Only Preserve Life Forms

Changes in basic kinds are limited to variations within the kinds. Harmful mutations lead to extinction, not to new complex systems. Mutations cannot create a single gene.

Plants and animals were originally created with large gene pools within their created kinds. A large gene pool gives a created kind the genetic potential (the potential to produce a variety of types within a kind) to adapt to various ecosystems and ensure the survival of that kind of organism through natural selection.

Genetic potential can best be understood by observing the large number of dog breeds. There are many shapes, sizes, and colors of dogs, illustrating the tremendous genetic potential in this kind of animal. Other kinds of plants and animals have similar potential to produce variety within a created kind. Natural selection can only operate on the genetic material already present in a population of organisms. It cannot create new genetic information and subsequently change one kind of organism into another.

Man Was Recently and Miraculously Created in the Image of God

The first human beings did not evolve from an animal ancestry, but were specially created in fully human form from the start.

What separates man from the animal kingdom? Although human genetics and human appearance are different from any animal, there are less apparent, but more important, reasons that determine the nature of man than just his genome.

Genesis 1 reveals that man was created in the image of God, a quality that separates him from the animals created on Day Six. This special creation explains why man's behavior is far more complex than any other living thing on the planet. Man reveals God's image in many ways. For example:

- Man is able to imagine and make objects never seen before.
- Man is able to show compassion for strangers.
- Man is able to ponder his role and fate in creation.

Man also differs from the other creatures in his relationship to God. Man was created to serve other men and God, a fact that forms the basis for society. Men are God's most treasured creation. God treasures man so much that He died to reconcile man to Himself. It is this value that God places on man that truly separates him from the rest of creation. What really distinguishes man from the animals is the decision each man will make in response to God's provision for salvation.

All People Descended Recently from a Single Family

The first human beings, Adam and Eve, were specially created by God, and all other men and women are their descendants. Mitochondria are organelles in the cells of every human that carry a small amount of DNA. Mitochondria are inherited solely through the egg from the mother, allowing the identification of descendants from any female lineage. Variations in mitochondrial DNA between people have conclusively shown that all people have descended from one female, just as it is stated in Scripture.

The instability of the mitochondrial genome and computer simulations modeling mutation load in humans indicate that the human mitochondrial genome is very young, which fits within a biblical time frame.

Y chromosomes are passed on to sons from their father, and just as mitochondrial DNA shows that all have descended from one female, Y chromosome analysis suggests that all men have descended from one common male ancestor.

Humans Are Stewards with Purpose and Accountability

Mankind was instructed to care for all other created organisms, and over the earth itself. The Creator's commission includes science, technology, commerce, fine art, and education. Man has dominion over the earth, but that dominion cannot exceed the boundaries of God's laws, meaning that we are stewards of God's creation.

Responsible environmental management includes consideration for the preservation of the ecosystem and provides for basic human needs. Such responsibility would include not engaging in reproductive technologies that intentionally destroy human life or create human life for experimentation. Or application of biotechnology to provide relief from human suffering, while not encouraging human genetic or cybernetic enhancements that provide "superhuman" qualities.

Christ left an example by relieving human suffering around Him, but not providing enhancement to those who were not in need of healing. He did these things to bring glory to God and to reveal Himself as God's Son. He never performed miracles to glorify the disciples or others who surrounded Him. The disciples also followed this example and made it clear when they healed someone that God should be acknowledged for the deliverance.

FOR FURTHER STUDY

The articles listed below are available at www.icr.org. Find the "Search" bar on the opening page of the website, type in the title of the article that you wish to read, and click "Enter." The web search will take you directly to the article.

A Few Reasons an Evolutionary Origin of Life Is Impossible

Ammonite Evolution?

Are Fossils the Result of Noah's Flood?

Are Things Getting Better or Are They Running Down?

Basic Chemistry: A Test of Creation

Bursting Big Bang's Bubble

Can Order Come Out of Chaos?

Can Raw Energy Create Order?

Carbon Dating Undercuts Evolution's Long Ages

Confirmation of Rapid Metamorphism of Rocks

Cosmology on Trial

Creating the Missing Link: A Tale About a Whale

Creation and Quantum Mechanics

Creation Cosmologies Solve Spacecraft Mystery

Creation, Selection, and Variation

Curiously Wrought

Debating Design: The Bacterial Flagellum

Did Noah's Flood Cover the Himalayan Mountains?

Did the African Eve Leave Footprints?

DNA: A Stew-pendous Creation

Do Millions of Laminae in the Green River Shales Document Millions of Years?

Does Entropy Contradict Evolution?

Does the Geologic Column Prove Evolution?

Don't the Fossils Prove Evolution?

Entropy and Open Systems

Evidence for a Young Earth from the Ocean and Atmosphere

Evidence for a Young World

Evolution and the Image of God

Evolution Hopes You Don't Know Chemistry: The Problem of Control

Evolution Is Biologically Impossible

Evolution Is Religion—Not Science

Evolution, Thermodynamics, and Entropy

Evolution: The Changing Scene

Evolution: The Ocean Says NO!

Finding an Evolutionist's God

Follow the Evidence!

Geology and the Flood

Has Evidence for the Flood Been Found in the Black Sea?

How Big Is God?

How Did the Vertical Columns at Devil's Tower Form?

How Long Did It Take to Deposit the Geologic Strata?

How Soon After the Flood Did the Earth Return to Equilibrium?

In His Pleasure

In the Beginning, Hydrogen

Irrational Naturalism

Lagerstätten!

Mankind—The Pinnacle of God's Creation

Microscopic Masterpieces: Discovering Design in Snow Crystals

Mimicry

Origin of Mankind

Production of Therapeutic Proteins by Genetic Engineering

Radiocarbon in "Ancient" Fossil Wood

Rapid Petrification of Wood: An Unexpected Confirmation of Creationist Research

EVIDENCE *from* SCRIPTURE

For ever, O LORD, thy word is settled in heaven.
Thy faithfulness is unto all generations:
thou hast established the earth, and it abideth.
Psalm 119:89-90

EVIDENCE *from* SCRIPTURE

S cripture clearly presents God as the Creator of all things. Not only is the opening of Genesis uniquely obvious, but the rest of Scripture is replete with the theme that the timeless God of eternity past created the universe.

It is no academic secret that the main proponents of evolutionary naturalism and the associated sociological exponents of that philosophy are atheistic in theory, if not in practice. All "modern," "postmodern," and the many variations of "scientism" are united in their opposition to the concept of a transcendent Creator God. The very idea of an omnipotent, omniscient Being is anathema to "naturalistic" concepts of existence.

The myriad pantheistic and polytheistic religious and spiritual "isms" of history, as well as the New Age proponents of today, all embrace some form of eternal matter with "long-age" and "gradual" development of the universe and life. The academic world has begun to entertain "spiritual" interpretations of naturalistic science as the evidence for complexity and design grows more and more obvious. Yet they all still cling to the evolutionary cosmologies.

Once again, we are faced with a philosophy, a certain interpretation of information, which is in diametrical opposition to the revealed text of Scripture. A "god" who would use the cruel, inefficient, wasteful, death-filled processes of the random, purposeless mechanisms of naturalistic evolution, contrasts so radically with the God described in the pages of the Bible that one wonders how the two characters can ever be thought to be in harmony.

We must either resolve the conflict or reject one of the two opposing views.

AUTHENTIC TEXT

The Bible's text is inspired by God in a way that used selected humans to write its original words (even to each letter in every word), resulting in the precise message that God intended for us to know. God also providentially ensured that this "Book of books" was satisfactorily transmitted and reproduced, so its transmitted text is authentic, as well as more plentifully distributed than any other book in earth's history.

Many powerful men over the centuries have tried to discredit or destroy the Bible. All have failed. There is more evidence for the authenticity and accuracy of the Scriptures than for any other ancient book. No one who has studied these issues doubts the genuineness of the Bible. Many, however, reject its message.

The Manuscripts

There are more hand-copied manuscripts of the Bible in existence than for any other book. There is more evidence for the Bible's authenticity than for any literature of antiquity. Textual analysis begins with historical investigation, beginning with the latest documents and working backward. As evidence develops, the data is evaluated against other sources. The record is then checked for consistency of information, and the claims are analyzed as if it were a legal case, looking for credible testimony with cross-examination. There is an enormous amount of evidence for authenticity of the biblical manuscripts.

The New Testament was written in the first century A.D. There are some 20,000 manuscripts in existence. The earliest textual evidence we have was copied 100 years after the original. In contrast:

- Caesar's *Gallic Wars* was written in the first century B.C. There are only 10 manuscripts in existence. The earliest textual evidence we have was copied 1,000 years after the original.

- Aristotle's *Poetics* was written in the fourth century B.C. There are only 5 manuscripts in existence. The earliest textual evidence we have was copied 1,400 years after the original.

There are many more writings of the Church Fathers quoting sections of Scripture; we could reconstruct the entire New Testament from their writings alone. There were millions of man-hours spent in cross-checking the manuscripts. There remains only 1 percent of all New Testament words about which questions still exist; no questionable passage contradicts any Bible teaching.

The Old Testament has been more accurately transmitted to us than any other ancient writing of comparable age. The textual evidence is greater for both the Old and New Testaments than any other historically reliable ancient document. The ancient scribes were very meticulous. There were only 1,200 variant readings in A.D. 500.

The Masorites produced an official text in A.D. 500. There are other versions that confirm the accuracy of the Masoritic Text.

- Samaritan Pentateuch: 400 B.C.
- Septuagint Greek: 280 B.C.
- Dead Sea Scrolls: 0 A.D.
- Latin Vulgate: 400 A.D.

The quotations from pre-Christian writing confirm the text. The New Testament accepts the Old Testament as authentic, confirming the traditional authors, quoting from at least 320 different passages, and confirming the supernatural events cited in the Old Testament.

The Message

There are over 3,000 different religions in the world, all of which claim to teach the way to eternal happiness. It has often been said that each of them provides a different path to the same end, and that men are free to choose the path that best suits their own disposition and culture. The Word of God is insistent that this is not so!

The Bible insists that the God of the Bible is the only true God (Isaiah 44:6; 45:5-6) and that Jesus Christ is the only way to God (John 14:6). All other religions, while stressing their "paths," would allow for some other contingency.

The Bible insists that it is the only true revelation, that its words are not to be changed (Proverbs 30:5-6; Revelation 22:18-19), and that its words are the basis of all judgment (John 12:47-50).

The Bible has a unique account of origins (Genesis 1-11). All others are either evolutionary or pantheistic, with eternity of matter as the "beginning." The biblical account of origins is unique in both quality and quantity of information.

The Bible has a unique historical basis. Other religions are based on the subjective teachings of their founders. Biblical teachings are based on objective and demonstrable facts: creation, the fall, the Flood, the life and work of redemption of Christ.

Creation Was 24/6 and Recent

The most controversial book of the Bible is Genesis, especially the first eleven chapters. Those chapters speak of the creation of the universe, the fall of man into sin, the worldwide Flood of Noah, and the language-altering event at Babel. There is much evidence that these events are historically accurate.

Although some would suggest that the biblical account of creation is either allegorical or analogous to the evolutionary story, the text itself does not permit such an application.

The language of Genesis chapters 1 and 2 are technically precise and linguistically clear. Any reader would understand that the author of those pages intended to convey a normal six-day creation, involving God's supernatural intervention both to create (something from nothing) and to make and shape (something basic into something more complex).

Three days (Day 1, Day 5, and Day 6) involve creation. Three days (Day 2, Day 3, and Day 4) involve the organization, integration, and structuring of the material created on Day 1.

Life was created on Day 5, a life in which all animals and man share. A special image of God was created on Day 6 that only man has. The movement from "simple to complex" may appear to follow evolution's theory, but the specific order (water > land > plants > stellar and planetary bodies > birds and fish > land animals > man) most emphatically does not.

The Hebrew word for day (*yom*) is used some 3,000 times in the Hebrew Bible, and is almost always used to mean an ordinary 24-hour day-night cycle. On the few occasions where it is used to mean an indeterminate period of time, it is always clear from the context that it means something other than a 24-hour day (day of trouble, day of the Lord, day of battle, etc). Whenever it is used with an ordinal (1, 2, 1st, 2nd, etc.), it always means a specific day, an ordinary 24-hour day.

The language of Genesis 1 appears to have been crafted so that no reader would mistake the word use for anything other than an ordinary 24-hour day. The light portion is named "day," and the dark portion is named "night." Then the "evening and the morning" is Day 1, Day 2, etc. The linguistic formula is repeated for each of the six days, a strange emphasis if the words were to be taken as allegorical or analogous to something other than a day-night cycle.

When God wrote the Ten Commandments with His own finger (certainly the most emphatic action ever taken by God on behalf of His revealed Word), God specifically designated a seventh day to be a "Sabbath" day (rest day) in memory and in honor of the work-six-days, rest-one-day activity of God during the creation week (Exodus 20:11). In that context, spoken and written by God Himself, the creation week can mean only a regular week of seven days, one of which is set aside as holy.

Sin Caused Death

The biblical record is very precise: Adam's sin introduced death into the world (Genesis 3:17; Romans 5:12), with death being the "last enemy" (1 Corinthians 15:26). Naturalistic interpretations must have death as a good mechanism that produces the "most fit."

A major platform of those who hold to the long ages of formative biology is that death is a normal part of the original creation. The position is that the fossil remains are a record of eons of natural development rather than the awful debris of a worldwide, year-long sentence of destruction executed by an angry Creator.

The Bible insists, however, that death is an enemy (1 Corinthians 15:26), a curse (Genesis 3:14-17) pronounced on all creation, including living creatures. That awful judgment was because of Adam's rebellion (Genesis 3:17; 1 Timothy

2:14) and was not a part of God's good creation.

Death by the design of God is so foreign to the revealed nature of God, one is at a loss to understand why anyone would want to suggest that God "authored" death in His creation, a creation that was designed to tell us of His invisible nature and Godhead. The whole message of Scripture turns on Genesis 3. All of the "good" of the environment was withdrawn with God's sentence. The "groaning and travailing" (Romans 8:22) began at that moment, or the words of God Himself are void!

If there were eons of pain, suffering, and death before the rebellion of Adam brought death into the world, then a whole sweep of biblical teaching is thrown into the black hole of allegory. Hundreds of Bible passages are twisted from a warning and a bad consequence to a "normal" event. In the Bible, physical death is specifically identified as absolutely necessary to accomplish the atonement for sins.

There is no question that the Bible teaches that it was necessary for Jesus Christ to die physically in order to accomplish the payment for our sins (Hebrews 2:14-18). If death is normal and/or good, even if it is merely relegated to a "spiritual" effect, then the physical death of Jesus Christ becomes unnecessary and meaningless.

Necessary Redemption

The Bible teaches a unique plan of redemption. It reveals a unique Savior.

- He was born of a virgin (Isaiah 7:14; Matthew 1:18-25).
- He lived a sinless life (Hebrews 4:14-16).
- He taught as no other man taught (John 7:46; Matthew 7:28-29).
- He died a unique, volitional death (John 10:17-18; Luke 23:46).
- He had unique victory over death (Acts 17:31; 1 Corinthians 15:3-8).

The Bible demands a unique salvation.

- Perfect holiness is required (Romans 3:10-18, 23; 6:23).
- Substitutionary atonement is the only means of reconciliation (Hebrews 10:4-14; Romans 3:24-26).
- Grace is the only measurement (Ephesians 2:8-10; Romans 11:5-6).

Other religions require some form of works or participation.

ACCURATE DATA

The information contained in the Bible is holy, and it is wholly accurate, too. When the Bible mentions a scientific topic, it is scientifically accurate. Likewise, the Bible is historically accurate, mathematically accurate, etc.

The Bible is unique among all books. Not only is it different in its form, structure, and history, but it takes the position of supernatural superiority to all other communication. It insists on total accuracy for its content and absolute obedience to its commands. No other book is so demanding.

Biblical Data Is Testable

Historical evidence routinely includes ancient literature, business records, and government documents, analyzed in conjunction with linguistics, geography, and archaeological analysis of physical objects (pottery, coins, remains of buildings, etc.), using forensic science techniques. After many millions of man-hours of research and evidence analysis, archaeology has repeatedly confirmed the reliability of the Bible. The Bible has been proven geographically and re-proven historically accurate, in the most exacting detail, by external evidences.

Historical Accuracy

The biblical record is full of testable historical and archaeological data, unlike the sacred texts of other religions. Wherever such historical information is cited, the data has proven to be precise and trustworthy.

The Bible has proven to be more historically and archaeologically accurate than any other ancient book. It has been subjected to the minutest scientific textual analysis possible to humanity and has been proven to be authentic in every way.

The Bible has become a significant source book for secular archaeology, helping to identify such ancient figures as Sargon (Isaiah 20:1); Sennacherib (Isaiah 37:37); Horam of Gazer (Joshua 10:33); Hazar (Joshua 15:27); and the nation of the Hittites (Genesis 15:20). The biblical record, unlike other "scriptures," is historically set, opening itself up for testing and verification.

Two of the greatest 20th-century archaeologists, William F. Albright and Nelson Glueck, both lauded the Bible (even though they were non-Christian and secular in their training and personal beliefs) as being the single most accurate source document from history. Over and over again, the Bible has been found to be accurate in its places, dates, and records of events. No other "religious" document comes even close.

The 19th-century critics used to deny the historicity of the Hittites, the Horites, the Edomites, and various other peoples, nations, and cities mentioned in the Bible. Those critics have long been silenced by the archaeologist's spade, and few critics dare to question the geographical and ethnological reliability of the Bible.

The names of over 40 different kings of various countries mentioned in the Bible have all been found in contemporary documents and inscriptions outside of the Old Testament, and are always consistent with the times and places associated with them in the Bible. Nothing exists in ancient literature that has been even remotely as well-confirmed in accuracy as has the Bible.

Scientific Accuracy

The Bible is not a science textbook, but it does deal with scientifically relevant issues. Although much controversy surrounds the early chapters of Genesis, empirical (observable, testable, repeatable) science verifies the Bible's information.

Many would suggest that the Bible is an antiquated religious book, filled with scientific fallacies and mistakes. Others believe that the Bible is a book of true religion, but dealing solely with spiritual subjects, with any matters of science and history to be interpreted spiritually or allegorically.

Either the Bible is wholly reliable on every subject with which it deals, or it is not the Word of God. Although the Bible is obviously not a science textbook (otherwise it would be continuously out of date), the Bible does contain all the basic principles upon which true science is built. The Bible abounds with references to nature and natural processes, and thus frequently touches on the various sciences.

For instance, there are many passages that deal with principles of hydrology, geology, astronomy, meteorology, biology, physics, cosmology, and the grand principles of the space-mass/energy-time continuum.

Again, if the God revealed in the Bible truly exists, then everything that He reveals would of necessity be true.

One often hears of mistakes or errors in the Bible. Seldom, when confronted, is there an example provided. When such "errors" are cited, they fall into three kinds of alleged mistakes: 1) mathematical rounding, 2) relative motion, or 3) miracles. Obviously, mathematical rounding is both scientific and in constant use today, as is the use of relative motion for all sorts of navigation and distance calculations. To deny the miraculous is to assume that one is omniscient.

Just as the Bible has become a source book for history and archaeology, so it is also a source book for the foundational principles of science. Those who ignore the information of Scripture will be "ever learning, and never able to come to the knowledge of the truth" (2 Timothy 3:7).

Plants and Animals Are Distinct

In the Creator's design, plants were made for food and animals were living evidence of the Creator's wonder and diversity. There is no hint, of course, in the Genesis account that God equated the replicating systems of earth with the living creatures later created on days 5 and 6. Much has been written to justify this equation, but neither the Scriptures nor science supports it. There is a vast difference between the most complex plant and the simplest living organism. If one uses the biblical distinction (blood, Leviticus 17:11) as the wall between plant and animal, the differences are even greater.

There is no question that God created the various categories of grass, herbs, and fruit-bearing plants. The gulf between "dirt" and "plants" is huge! No naturalistic scheme can adequately account for such wonder. But according to God's words, they do not have "life." Plants do replicate within their kind, but so do certain crystals and some chemicals. They replicate within kind, but they are nowhere said to possess *chay* (life) or *nephesh* (soul), the Hebrew words for living things. Job 14:8-10 is cited as evidence that plants die like people die, but that passage most certainly does not use the words for life. The supposed comparison is really a contrast between plant and man.

The food created by God as a "good" product and part of the process to maintain life cannot be equated with the awful sentence of death pronounced by the Creator on His creation. Animals and man have life. Plants do not.

The Flood Was Global

The language of Genesis 6-9 demands that the great Flood of Noah be understood as a planet-covering, geologically destructive, year-long water cataclysm. That global flooding left enormous evidence of the event.

There is a great divide between two major systems of belief on the biblical Flood in the days of Noah. There are those who say it is either a purely mythological event or else possibly a local or regional flood. Then there are those who accept the biblical record of the Flood as a literal record of a tremendous cataclysm involving not only a worldwide deluge, but also great tectonic upheavals and volcanic outpourings that completely changed the crust of the earth and its topography in the days of Noah.

Jesus Christ believed the Old Testament record of the worldwide Flood. Speaking of the antediluvian population, He said: "The flood came, and took them all away" (Matthew 24:39).

Evolutionary anthropologists are all convinced that people had spread over the entire earth by the time assigned to Noah in biblical chronology, so an anthropologically universal Flood would clearly have required a geographically worldwide Flood.

The apostle Peter believed in a worldwide hydraulic cataclysm. "Whereby the world [Greek *kosmos*] that then was, being overflowed [Greek *katakluzo*] with water, perished" (2 Peter 3:6). The world was defined in the previous verse as "the heavens...and the earth." Peter also said that "God...spared not the old world, but saved Noah…bringing in the flood [Greek *kataklusmos*] upon the world of the ungodly" (2 Peter 2:5).

The Old Testament record of the Flood, which both Christ and Peter accepted as real history, clearly teaches a global Flood. For example, the record emphasizes that "all the high hills, that were under the whole heaven…and the mountains were covered" (Genesis 7:19-20) with the waters of the Flood.

Since "all flesh died that moved upon the earth…all that was in the dry land" (Genesis 7:21-22), Noah and his sons had to build a huge Ark to preserve animal life for the postdiluvian world, an Ark that can easily be shown to have had more than ample capacity to carry at least two of every known species of land animal (marine animals were not involved, of course). Such an Ark was absurdly unnecessary for anything but a global Flood.

God promised that never "shall there any more be a flood to destroy the earth" (Genesis 9:11), and He has kept His word for over 4,000 years, if the Flood indeed was global. Those Christians who say it was a local flood, however, are in effect accusing God of lying, for there are many devastating local floods every year.

Reliable Eyewitnesses

The information available about the 40 authors of the biblical text clearly demonstrates both their historicity and their credibility. Many of these writers were well known in secular history, and many suffered cruelly while defending the accuracy of their material.

The Bible, like many books, was written by eyewitnesses (Luke 1:2; 2 Peter 2:16) to the events and circumstances that they recorded. That they were trustworthy witnesses is only to be expected, since God inspired them to co-author their respective portions of the Bible. But some ask: How can we know if the Bible's human co-authors were really reliable eyewitnesses?

The following eyewitness traits are the ones emphasized in common law, in law school, and in the Rules of Evidence.

A reliable witness will evidence honesty by his/her sincerity of speech, and be clearly motivated by a drive to speak the truth. The quality of a witness's observations can be observed by accurate memory, evidenced often by access to accurate records. The competency of his/her communication will be demonstrated by an ability to recall and describe observations, with accurate information and relevant details. Testimonial consistency is also a key factor in reliability.

Though each witness will provide idiosyncratic differences (due to different perspectives and interests), all Scripture has perfect evidentiary consistency. Matthew, Mark, Luke, John, Paul, Moses, Daniel, Jude, and all of the other Bible's co-authors qualify as impeccably reliable eyewitnesses. Many of the Bible's writers suffered cruel treatment, even death, for their stand on their witness. To the obvious credibility of their writings is added the unshakeable belief that their testimony was so true that it was worth suffering and dying for.

ASSESSABLE RESULTS

The Bible stands up to being tested, like an anvil beaten by many hammers. The Bible proves that it is God's Word by its prediction of events, beyond all possible odds, that are now documented history, including the prophesied events about Jesus as the predicted Messiah, as well as providing the witness of lives transformed as only the Bible indicated would occur.

Transformed Lives

History is replete with testimonies of radically changed lives. The Bible speaks of a "new creature" (2 Corinthians 5:17), "created in righteousness and true holiness" (Ephesians 4:24). Such transformation is classic evidence of the power of God.

The message that permeates the Bible is that all humans are sinful by their nature and conscious action, and are under the judgment of a holy and righteous Creator-God, who has willing offered His own Son as the substitutionary sacrifice for humanity's sentence of eternal death. That salvation transforms! The "new birth" is a "new creation." Such a supernatural event must transform a life, if it is real. Both the Bible and history are replete with such evidence.

- Pagan Abram (later Abraham) believed God (Galatians 6:3) and became the "father of many nations" (Genesis 17:5).

- Banished Jacob (Genesis 27:43) became a "prince" with the name Israel (Genesis 32:28).

- Joseph, despised and hated by his brothers, became the ruler in Egypt "to save much people alive" (Genesis 50:20).

- Moses the murderer became Moses the deliverer (Exodus 3:10).

- Gideon the fearful became Gideon the mighty man of valor (Judges 6:12).

- Samuel the child became Samuel the judge (1 Samuel 7:15).

- David the shepherd became David the giant-killer (1 Samuel 17:45) and king (2 Samuel 7:8).

- Zacchaeus the dishonest tax collector became Zacchaeus the generous benefactor (Luke 19:8).

- Peter the rough commercial fisherman became a "fisher of men" (Matthew 4:19).

- Saul the self-righteous Pharisee and persecutor of Christians (Acts 9:1) became Paul the Apostle and teacher of the Gentiles (2 Timothy 1:11).

Every book of the Bible contains records of such transformations, as does every era of history. From the coliseum in Rome and the persecutions during the Middle Ages to the wonderful conversions of the addicts and outcasts of society, as well as the quiet and simple response of the child who seeks to return the love of Jesus, all testify to the transforming power of the Gospel.

Accurate Predictions

The Bible contains many, many prophetic predictions, most of which are quite detailed. Either they come true, or they do not. If one prediction is accurate, it might be called coincidence. When dozens (even hundreds) come true, the odds become astronomical.

The purpose of prophecy in the Bible is given in Isaiah 46:9-10:

> I am God, and there is none like me, declaring the end from the beginning, and from ancient times the things that are not yet done.

Supernatural predictions are evidence provided to us for verification. Not a single prophecy from the Bible has been proven false. Many prophecies remain in the future, but all that have come to pass have been verified to be true. Thousands of prophecies from the Bible have been fulfilled.

An amazing prophecy is found in Revelation 11:9. In 90 A.D., the prediction was made that many nations would view the same event within a few days time. Today, billions of people from around the world simultaneously view the same event through mass communication. When the prediction was made, communication and transportation across the Roman Empire took months of time.

In 332 B.C., Alexander the Great conquered the island fortress of Tyre by building a causeway from the ruins of the old city. This fulfilled the prophecy in Ezekiel 26:4-5, written hundreds of years before. At the time of Ezekiel, Tyre was the capital of Phoenicia and the island fortress had not yet been built. Ezekiel predicted:

> They shall destroy the walls of Tyre, and break down her towers: I will also scrape her dust from her, and make her like the top of a rock. It shall be a place for the spreading of nets in the midst of the sea.

Two hundred years later, Alexander scraped away everything, leaving bare rock.

And, of course, there are hundreds of fulfilled prophesies related to the birth, life, death, and resurrection of Jesus Christ.

Contrasting Worldviews

The obvious "good and evil" conflict in every culture throughout all recorded time is clearly articulated and explained in the Bible. Buried deep in the human psyche are timeless questions, questions that surface frequently and suddenly throughout one's lifetime. Every person capable of rational thought thinks these things. There are no exceptions. There are no exclusions.

- Who am I? (identity)
- Why am I here? (purpose)
- What is going to happen to me? (future, life after death)
- Where did I come from, and how and when did all this start? (origins)

No human being operates without a bias, a predisposition to believe one idea over another. In religious terms we would call that bias "faith."

The naturalist believes that there is no supernatural force in existence and that man has reached the stage in eternity where he is able to direct the evolutionary development of the universe.

The creationist believes that a Creator God exists and that the creatures of that God must seek to understand His will.

The common data that both believers share will be interpreted in the light of the belief system (worldview, faith) that the individual holds. When we ask the questions that plague our minds (Why is the world so full of evil? Or, why can't we all get along? Or, why can't we seem to get "enough"? Or, is it always going to be this way?), the answers come from our worldview. What we believe will frame our reactions, our priorities, and our expectations.

The Bible describes the many facets of belief systems (worldviews) in their simplest and most fundament form: truth or lie.

The ultimate contrast is between the revelation of the Creator-God who cannot lie (Hebrews 6:18) and the great adversary, Satan, who is the "father" of the lie (John 8:44). The Bible provides a comprehensive and logically consistent body of answers and explanations to all of the critical worldview issues: who (including Who), what, where, when, how, and why. In fact, the Bible even has an explanation for why we have such different viewpoints on the critical worldview issues. The Bible also predicts cause-and-effect connections between the kind of worldview we have, the kind of actions we take in life, and the impact of those actions, both here and in the hereafter.

Human Stewardship

The first command given to humanity was to "rule" and "subdue" and "have dominion" over the earth. That delegated authority contains the fundamental warrant for all human endeavors, as stewards of earth. This Dominion Mandate, found in Genesis 1:26-28, and later repeated and amplified to Noah (Genesis 9:1-7), is still in force as the Creator's authorization for humanity to be the stewards of earth.

The Dominion Mandate authorizes all honorable human occupations as a stewardship under God. God's first command to the man and woman He had created was to exercise dominion "over all the earth" (Genesis 1:26), not a despotic dominion, as some have insinuated, but a responsible stewardship.

In order to subdue the earth, we must first understand its processes. Thus, research is the foundational occupation for fulfilling the divine mandate. Then this knowledge must be applied in technology (engineering, medicine, agriculture, etc.). It must be implemented for use by all (business, commerce) and transmitted to future generations (education). The creation can also be described and praised in the humanities and fine arts.

The Dominion Mandate thus authorizes all honorable human occupations as a stewardship under God.

The Mandate was reaffirmed to Noah after the Flood (Genesis 9:1-10) with the additional institution of human government, a change made necessary by the entrance of sin and death into the world. Thus, all the occupations we now call the social sciences (law, civics, counseling, etc.) have been added to God's authorized vocations.

This all-encompassing command will be part of the great judgment when "the dead were judged out of those things which were written in the books, according to their works" (Revelation 20:12).

Science

The command to "subdue" first requires understanding the earth. The disciplines of science uncover how things work. In order for mankind to subdue the earth and have dominion over it, humanity would eventually have to occupy every region of it. Man was to keep the earth (Genesis 2:15), not exploit and waste its resources. The command to subdue does not imply that the earth was an enemy, but rather that it was a complex and wonderful world, to be ordered and controlled for man's benefit and God's glory.

Performing the function of subduing and exercising dominion over the physical and biological creations necessarily implies the development of physical and biological sciences (physics, chemistry, hydrology, etc., as well as biology, physiology, ecology, etc.) Thus, the work involved suggests the study and understanding of the created world, or, as Kepler and other great scientists have put it, "thinking God's thoughts after Him."

Since sin entered the world, profound changes have taken place in all of God's created domains. The ground itself was cursed (Genesis 3:17), as were the living creatures (Genesis 3:14). The principle of decay and disintegration began to operate in physical systems; mutations, disease, and death began to debilitate biological systems. No longer is science merely required to understand the function and organization of earth; it must now attempt to uncover the original designs of those processes and to learn how to repair the increasing damage being done.

Factual and quantitative data in all areas of study are accessible to all men with the capacity to pursue them. The interpretive and philosophical applications of such data, however, depend strongly on one's spiritual condition.

Technology

The command to "rule" requires effective use in the service of mankind. The disciplines of technology involve the development and application of all science.

Obedience to the Dominion Mandate also requires the concordant development of physical and biological technologies (engineering, agriculture, medicine, etc.). These activities under the stewardship of the Dominion Mandate imply the complementary enterprises known by the modern terms of science and technology, research and development, theory and practice, etc.

Technology, development, and practice suggest the application and utilization of the physical and biological processes and systems, as learned from their scientific study, for the benefit of mankind and the glory of God.

There have also arisen the social sciences (psychology, sociology, etc.) and their respective technologies for implementation in organized human societies (economics, government, politics, etc.), so that these fields now also come within the bounds of the Dominion Mandate and thus are proper disciplines.

As with scientific research, factual and quantitative data in all areas of study is most accurate and useful in technological development. The interpretive and philosophical applications, however, are either tainted or enhanced by one's spiritual condition.

Commerce

The command to "fill the earth" also involves distributing the "useful" things to everyone.

Implied in the great Dominion Mandate is the necessity of distribution. Science is charged with the responsibility of researching the forces and processes of the earth to determine how things function. Technology is delegated the task of developing useful tools and techniques for the application of the information gained in research. Commerce (business) is the complementary discipline necessary to distribute the "useful things" to everyone.

In essence, commerce is complying with the "fill the earth" portion of the mandate. Adam and Eve were placed in the Garden and told to "dress and keep" it. They were not told how to do so, only that it was their responsibility before the Creator to maintain and develop what had been provided for them. As the population of earth grew, it would be necessary to develop skills to make their tools and talents available to others. That procedure in modern terms is "commerce."

There are a number of commerce-related instructions throughout the Scriptures. We are told not to be "slothful in business" but "fervent in spirit; serving the Lord" (Romans 12:11). Someone who is "diligent in his business" will "stand before kings; he shall not stand before mean men" (Proverbs 22:29). In one sense, business (commerce) is the familial responsibility of every person, and we are told to "study to be quiet, and to do your own business, and to work with your own hands" (1 Thessalonians 4:11).

Given the somewhat sordid reputation of business in general, it would be well if all commerce would heed the Golden Rule: "And as ye would that men should do to you, do ye also to them likewise (Luke 6:31). There is no doubt that those words were intended to be implemented by humanity when the mandate to "fill the earth" was first given.

Education

The knowledge of science, the skills of technology, and the techniques of commerce must be transmitted to others. It is important that true knowledge and wisdom, once known, not be either lost or corrupted. Each generation, therefore, has the responsibility to transmit its knowledge of truth, undiluted and undistorted, to the succeeding generation. This is the ministry of teaching.

In God's economy, the primary responsibility for educating the young is in the home (Deuteronomy 6:6-7; 2 Timothy 3:15; Ephesians 6:4). The churches also bear a complementary and extended responsibility to identify and equip God-called teachers as needed for all aspects of its educational ministries (1 Timothy 3:15). It is significant that there is no reference in the Scriptures to the school as a separate institution established by God.

That fact does not necessarily mean that parents and pastors have to do all the actual work of teaching. It is certainly appropriate for them to employ qualified tutors and trainers, but the control of the educational process should remain primarily with the home and secondarily with the church. The gift of teaching is identified in all three Bible lists of the gifts of the Spirit (Romans 12:1-8; 1 Corinthians 12:1-31; Ephesians 4:7-16). This gift focuses on the teaching of the Scriptures, of course. However, we must not forget that the

Bible provides the framework for all teaching. All physical, biological, and spiritual reality is created and maintained by God in Christ and revealed by the Spirit. All teaching, no matter how profound, attractive, or eloquent, should be tested by its fidelity to the Word of God.

Thus, the wonderful three-fold goal of teaching must be as follows:

- to transmit the truth in fullness and purity
- to train the student with love and wisdom
- to glorify Christ, in whom perfect love and absolute truth will be united forever

Humanities

The recording of man's achievements through literature, drama, art, etc., should all redound to God's glory. The humanities and fine arts are the spiritual and emotional extension of the knowledge and technological state of society. While the disciplines of science and technology are fairly grounded in factual and quantitative data, the farther one gets from that which is "true" to that which is "applied," the more likely the sin nature will distort or contaminate the discipline.

That contamination affects the humanities and fine arts in even greater measure. These professions cannot even use the empirical data developed by secular persons, as can be done with the social sciences, because there are practically no empirical data involved in the humanities and fine arts.

In this realm, practically everything is based on either human reasoning or emotions, with the exception of the actual mechanical techniques of writing, composing, painting, or performing. But reasoning and emotions come from the mind and heart which, in the secular person, are without the benefit of the godly mind (2 Corinthians 2:14).

As the world has advanced, the growing secularization of society has increased. This is relatively easy to observe in the great art museums of our large cities. As one moves from the older galleries to the modern galleries, the movement of art from realism to abstract and from godly to profane is easy to see. One does not have to be an art critic to observe the trends.

Perhaps it would be helpful for the Christian person to remember: "Whether therefore ye eat, or drink, or whatsoever ye do, do all to the glory of God" (1 Corinthians 10:31).

Government and Politics

The authorization for capital punishment entails the ultimate oversight of human relations through government, politics, sociology, indeed, all legitimate human endeavors. In God's renewal of the Dominion Mandate to Noah after the Flood (Genesis 9:6-7), man was given the institution of human government, as epitomized in the authority to impose capital punishment as the penalty for murder. This ultimate in governmental authority, of course, implies also that human government was now responsible to regulate other human interrelationships as well, since uncontrolled, self-centered activities could otherwise quickly lead to violence, murder, and even anarchy.

Law defines how governments and people should interact. Almost all laws are derived from the biblical Ten Commandments, both directly and in extrapolated applications of the implications. This is especially true of the last six of the commandments, those that deal directly with man's relationship to his fellow man.

Politics describes how governments and people actually interact, especially over money and power. Governmental institutions, which include our legal systems, are a mix of law and politics. This is partially because of their use of persuasive pressure (and enforceability) of law to influence the actual behavior of others.

American politics was mostly founded on Bible-friendly political principles by creationist patriots (most of whom were Bible-revering Protestants, as the U.S. Supreme Court once admitted). Many judges now view law itself as inherently secular and "evolving."

With evolutionary law-based politics, no one's basic rights are really secure, because political rights once deemed absolute and inalienable (such as a baby's right to be born, or a family's right to its homestead unless the property is taken for a truly "public" purpose) are now treated with arbitrariness, as if those rights were mere privileges that governments may take at will.

To the extent that government officials no longer respect God as the ultimate Authority, they functionally substitute their own power for His, using the evolutionary logic that "might makes right" instead of the Bible-friendly rule-of-law logic that "right justifies might."

Environment and Ecology

One part of governance under the Dominion Mandate is the understanding of earth and its inhabitants, weather, and other environmental factors that combine into the interactive whole and parts of what we call earth's ecology.

In Eden, and again after the Flood, mankind was commanded by God to exercise a steward's dominion over all the earth, including its many life forms, land animals, sea animals, birds, etc. This is a God-ordained mandate for the whole human race, in conjunction with God's decree that humans "be fruitful and multiply." To obey this mandate, mankind must understand earth and its inhabitants, weather, and other environmental factors that combine into the interactive whole and parts of what we call earth's ecology.

Ecology is the study of the ongoing interrelatedness of all of earth's life forms (including humans and the huge variety of animals, plants, bacteria, etc.) with all of the physical (i.e., non-living) environmental elements like soil, air, water, etc.

How do fish live in the sea? How do birds fly in the air? How and why do some animals seasonally migrate, or hibernate, or postpone gestation?

Mankind has God-assigned authority to use, consume, and otherwise manage animals, plants, and the physical environment (such as diverting river water for irrigation, harnessing wind power for sailing and windmills, or using rock for buildings). But this authority is a stewardship, requiring selfishness-restrictive rules, wise agriculture, and conservation.

Man's dominion (i.e., rule or management) is only right if and when it accords with God's revealed will for planet earth. Moral standards for doing that are found in the Bible.

Ethics and Justice

Ethics and justice should be complementary, ensuring both the moral and legal rightness of mankind's choices and actions. What should be the standard for how we determine right and wrong?

Ethics concerns what is morally right or wrong. Justice concerns what is legally right or wrong. Ideally, justice is ethical, and one assumes that doing what is ethical is legal. Justice cares about people's rights, and righting wrongs when those rights are violated. Although Cain denied being his "brother's keeper," we expect ethical standards and administered justice to function as a "brother's keeper" to someone (especially ourselves).

Justice can be restorative (compensatory), requiring the wrongdoer to restore the innocent victim, to the extent possible, to the same (or a similar) condition the victim was in before the wrong was committed (such as paying to repair damaged property, paying hospital bills, returning stolen goods, etc.). Or, justice can be punitive (penal), punishing the criminals, as a matter of social morality, for the wrong committed (involving jail time, fines, loss of a driver's license, a criminal record, or even capital punishment).

But sometimes the boundaries of what is morally right (ethical), individually and/or socially, are controversial. What about cloning, or artificial insemination, or various forms of contraception? What about informing human subjects that they are being experimented on for scientific or marketing research purposes? What about the use of deception by government officials (rationalized as required for national security, or to avoid a riot, or to promote a "social injustice" policy)?

What about civil rights, discrimination, and the persecution of Christians?

The Bible provides knowable answers to all of these moral decision-making questions, either directly or indirectly. The Bible's moral values are not like relativistic situational ethics. The Bible provides moral absolutes such as "thou shalt not steal," "thou shalt not murder," and "as ye would that men should do to you, do ye also to them likewise."

FOR FURTHER STUDY

The articles listed below are available at www.icr.org. Find the "Search" bar on the opening page of the website, type in the title of the article that you wish to read, and click "Enter." The web search will take you directly to the article.

The Creationism of America's Founding Fathers

The Deity of the Risen Christ

The Discerner

The Fall, the Curse, and Evolution

The Finished Works of God

The Flight of Migratory Birds

The Heavens are the Lord's

The Honest Apostles

The Impact of Evolution on the Humanities and Science

The Importance of Creationism in Foreign Missions

The Improbability of the Incarnation

The Light of the World

The Meaning of "Day" in Genesis

The New Age and Global Education

The New State Religion: Atheism

The Old Paths and the Good Way

The One True God?

The Principles of Creationism

The Tree of Life

The Ultimate Proof of Christianity

The Unjust Steward

The Ways and Works of God

The Year 2000 and Bible Prophecy

Thinking God's Thoughts After Him

This Is a "Taxing" Time

UCSD Scientist Discusses Evolution, Presents No New Defenses

When Messiah Came

Who Could Argue with Teaching Good Science?

Who Is Jesus Christ? A Challenge to Christians

Why?

About the Author

Henry M. Morris III serves as Chief Executive Officer of the Institute for Creation Research in Dallas, Texas. A former pastor, college professor and administrator, and business executive, Dr. Morris holds a D.Min. from Luther Rice Seminary and an M.B.A. from Pepperdine University.

The eldest son of ICR's founder, Dr. Morris is a popular conference and seminar speaker on the topics of biblical authority, the creation-evolution controversy, and the Christian worldview. A frequent guest on the nationally-syndicated radio programs *Back to Genesis* and *Science, Scripture & Salvation*, he is also the author of numerous articles and books, including *After Eden* and *5 Reasons to Believe in Recent Creation*.

FOR MORE INFORMATION

Sign up for ICR's FREE publications!

Creation? Evolution? Intelligent Design?

Which theory is correct? Six days or six billion years? Does it matter?

Find out with your free subscription to *Acts & Facts* magazine from the people who ignited the creation science movement nearly 40 years ago—the Institute for Creation Research.

The Institute for Creation Research equips believers with evidence of the Bible's accuracy and authority through scientific research, educational programs, and media presentations, all conducted within a thoroughly biblical framework.

Our monthly *Acts & Facts* magazine offers fascinating articles and current information on creation, evolution, and more. With your free subscription comes the complimentary *Days of Praise*, a quarterly booklet providing daily devotionals—real biblical "meat"—to strengthen and encourage the Christian witness.

Sign up for ICR's FREE publications today—call 800.337.0375, visit our website at www.icr.org, or write to the address below.

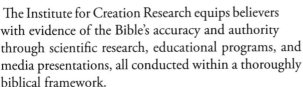

INSTITUTE
for CREATION
RESEARCH

P. O. Box 59029
Dallas, TX 75229
800.337.0375

FOR MORE INFORMATION

Visit ICR online

ICR.org offers a wealth of resources and information on scientific creationism and biblical worldview issues.

✓ Read our daily news postings on today's hottest science topics

✓ Explore the Evidence for Creation

✓ Investigate our graduate and professional education programs

✓ Dive into our archive of 40 years of scientific articles

✓ Listen to current and past radio programs

✓ Order creation science materials online

✓ And more!

For a free Resource Guide or to sign up for ICR's free publications, contact:

INSTITUTE for CREATION RESEARCH

P. O. Box 59029
Dallas, TX 75229
800.337.0375

Demand the Evidence.
Get it @ ICR.

www.icr.org